The Invisible Girl
A Memoir

Yvonne Sandomir

Legacy Book Press LLC
Camanche, Iowa

ACKNOWLEDGMENTS

Thank you to Lauren's Kids for its work on preventing child abuse and healing survivors, to which ten percent of the royalties from the sale of this book will be donated.

I would like to express my very great appreciation to two editors who helped me immensely throughout this process: Elizabeth Ridley, freelance editor with ServiceScape, and Heidi, also a freelance editor with ServiceScape. Thank you so much for helping me develop and structure my story to be the best it can be. I deeply appreciate your forethought and insightful assessment. I would also like to thank Rogelio Small with Blue Gem Productions. Thank you for all your efforts involved in this endeavor.

I offer a special thank you to my therapist, Laura. You are an angel on earth, and I'll be eternally grateful for all you've done to help me heal. Thank you from the bottom of my heart.

I am particularly grateful for my husband and his everlasting love, support, and comfort throughout this process. You're my rock, my best friend, and the love of my life. I love you SO much.

I am especially thankful for my mom, dad, brothers, and extended family. Thank you for being so supportive of this journey.

Finally, I wish to acknowledge my two daughters. Girlies, I love you more than words can express. I did it all for you.

DEDICATION

For the other 42+ million.

CONTENTS

TRIGGER WARNING

This book deals with child sexual abuse. While the author has taken great lengths to ensure the subject matter is dealt with in a compassionate and respectful manner, it may be troubling for some readers. Discretion is advised.

PREFACE

My biggest fear about sharing my story has always been what people will assume about me. It's terrifying to share such personal details about my life with strangers, but I realize it will be worth it in the end. I give you fair warning that my story includes material that won't be easy to read yet is relevant to ongoing issues in society. I genuinely believe my triumph over tragedy story will help others, because many people share these traumas with me.

My goal is to testify to the fact that even though we can't change the negative experiences we've endured, every one of us is capable of healing. Atrocious things happen to good people all the time, but it's possible to recover and learn how to stop self-sabotaging your healing efforts.

In June 2020, Lauren's Kids (www.laurenskids.org) reported that one out of three girls and one out of five boys in the United States alone will be victims of sexual abuse before their eighteenth birthdays. Shockingly, Lauren's Kids also estimates that seventy-five percent of victims don't report within the first year of their abuse. Forty-five percent of victims keep their abuse a secret for at least five years. Many stay silent for decades while many others never disclose their abuse at all.

These stats are not surprising, given that Lauren's Kids reports that ninety percent of abusers are people the children know, love, and trust, while thirty to forty percent of perpetrators are members of the victim's own family. These statistics are staggering, considering the same source also states it's possible to prevent ninety-five percent of child sexual abuse through education and awareness.

This horrifying data illustrates how prevalent child sexual abuse is across the United States. While sexual harassment and misconduct have become a focus of recent headlines, we hear about the epidemic of child sexual abuse and neglect less frequently.

I'm here to amplify the conversation, because there are millions of children suffering in silence among us. Child sexual abuse is a cancer of the soul that has metastasized throughout our society. These children grow up to join the "walking wounded," the more than forty-two million adult survivors of childhood sexual abuse and trauma in the United States, alone. Tragically, that number continues to increase, but with a dedicated support system and a diligent therapy regimen, there can be life after unimaginable childhood trauma.

Only now, in my forties, am I gaining the tools I need to dig out the distorted seeds my toxic environment planted in my psyche as a child. As a kid, I survived in an upside-down world where it was common to be around precarious people, destructive relationships, brutal domestic violence, sexual predators, and drug addiction. Due to my inhibited childhood, I'm an adult survivor of child abuse, family violence, sexual abuse, neglect, and multiple traumas.

I knew from an early age that the life my parents exposed me to would not be my life when I grew up. I believed with all my fragile heart that someday, no matter how difficult my circumstances, there would come a time for me to flee—and I did.

But, before a person gets to where they are going, they need to know from where they came. For most people who have a stable and supportive home life, it's easy to reminisce. But for others like me, recounting my history isn't a nostalgic process.

I've always known I'd have a story to tell. As the traumas started piling up in my adolescence and teenage years, I knew I was surviving horrendous acts committed against me that I'd write about someday, and here I am. This book is indeed an assemblage of my grisly traumas, but most importantly, it's representation of my long-fought journey to healing and true happiness.

Most people face tough decisions at some point in their lives, and I was no exception. When given a choice between fighting to make a difference or staying on a path of self-destruction, I chose to not only *make* a change but to *be* the change. "Making" the change is the physical act of changing behaviors. "Being" the difference is making a conscious effort to keep the momentum going every day.

If you remember nothing else from my journey, please remember this: It's okay to ask for help, it's okay to tell your story, and it's okay to feel all the things you don't want to feel. These are "normal" emotions in response to going through abnormal, traumatic experiences. I promise you that if you commit to getting the help you need, no matter what you've been through, you can heal from your past. But be prepared because it takes more than stepping into the therapist's office. It demands commitment, vulnerability, and enormous pain. I once thought that if I can do it, anyone can; however, with the help of therapy, I'm learning I've come as far as I have because of the time and effort I've put in.

A therapist isn't going to wave a magic wand and take your pain away. You must be willing to explore your deepest pain and work through it. There are many healthy ways to help. Whether it be through poetry, art, journaling, meditating, exercising, yoga, or singing, there are healthy outlets to release the emotions that will inevitably come when you begin the healing process. It won't be easy, but trust me when I tell you it's a journey worth traveling.

You'll learn that life is about making mistakes, detecting the lessons within, and understanding how to use that information to help you flourish. Everything I did as a child I did to survive.

Now, as an adult, I'm learning to thrive. I'm coming to terms with the fact that I'm a survivor, and I was a courageous and resilient child who did whatever she needed to do to survive a perilous childhood. Without my inner child, "Eve," I wouldn't be where I am today. Thanks to her, this invisible girl is coming out of the shadows.

I have changed the names, locations, and some situations to protect my family; however, everything else described is real and written as I remember the event.

This is my story.

CHAPTER ONE:
TRIGGERED

In February 2015, one month before my fairytale wedding to Gavin, a phone call with my mom changed my life forever.

It was late evening, around 8:00 p.m. Attempting to relax from a stressful day at the office, I ambled up the stairs to the master bedroom to rip off my ensemble of uncomfortable black stilettos and white belted sheath dress. My feet ached from touring the 60,000 sq. ft. resort from end to end with several pop-up clients that day. I kicked my heels off as soon as I entered the bedroom and plopped on the bed. I took a deep breath before falling back on the mattress. *Ugh, I wish I had a different haven to retreat to,* I thought as I looked around the cluttered 12x12 bedroom of our rental home.

Gavin's workstation was set up on the left side of the room, facing our headboard-less queen mattress and box spring. It took up a huge portion of the room. The television was placed in front of the bed on top of a small, wooden TV stand, and to the right was a fancy, full body massage chair covered with clean laundry that needed to be folded and put away. I took a deep breath. *Not today,* I quietly instructed myself. Even though our dresser was right next to the chair, the task felt too daunting to complete. I focused on the dull brown walls instead, imagining all the different colors I'd paint it if we owned the place. *Open air blue or a relaxing spa green would be lovely* I thought.

I stood up to unlatch the thin, black belt on my dress, dropping it to the floor as I stepped into the stark white master bathroom. *Do I want to shower right now? Nah,* I decided. I took off my dangly black and white teardrop earrings and dropped them into my jewelry box. I released my long, auburn hair from its restrictive bun, shook my head, and let my hair fall down my back. I moved back to our drab bedroom, unzipped my dress, and let it fall into a puddle on the floor. *Finally, I can get comfortable,* I thought, but then the phone rang. It was a rare phone call from my mom to discuss travel and lodging plans for Gavin's and my upcoming wedding.

"Hi, Mom, how are you?"

"I'm doing great, doll. I can't wait to see you in a few months."

"Same here, Mom. Did you get the hotel information I sent out?"

"I did, but that's what I'm calling about. I have concerns."

"Concerns? What concerns?"

"I just don't know that everybody can afford it is all."

"It's less than a hundred and fifty dollars a night. Can some people share a room?"

"Well, I was thinking a few people could pitch tents in your backyard."

"In my backyard? I don't see how that would work, Mom. We'll already have a house full. I just don't think it's appropriate."

"Ah hell, Eve, what's gotten into you? You've changed since you met Gavin."

"Mom, I can't talk anymore. I need to go." I hung up.

Gavin came upstairs when he heard the call getting heated, but he didn't make it until after I hung up. By that time, it was far too late. The dissatisfaction in Mama's voice triggered an event that never occurred before, and Gavin wasn't prepared for what happened next. According to Gavin, wearing only my bra and panties, I fell to the floor in a fetal position and began sobbing. He watched in bewilderment as I pulled my hair, and in a childlike voice, began recalling horrendous childhood traumas. It didn't last long, but I wasn't the same after. For the next few weeks leading up to our wedding, I began isolating myself in the bedroom for hours at a time and fell into a deep despair. I assumed things would improve after our wedding and romantic honeymoon, but sadly, things only got worse.

In March 2015, we celebrated our wedding and immediately took a ten-day long honeymoon to an all-inclusive resort in the Bahamas. Even with the stress of the wedding over and ten days in paradise to decompress, I felt no better than I did the day of the call. I was actually getting worse.

In May of 2015, Gavin, my husband of two short months, sat at the foot of the bed with the phone in his hand. He was casual in his black basketball shorts and "Rock, Paper, Scissor, Spock" tee shirt. The worried expression on his face didn't match the bright, sunny day we were having. Instead, it matched the darkness of the hideous light brown walls and lack of sunlight from our white blackout curtains. Gavin sat at his desk in the bedroom and took a deep breath before speaking.

"Yvonne, you need to see a therapist."

"Why are you doing this to me?" I snapped.

"Because I love you. That's why."

"Gavin, I don't need therapy. I promise I can do this on my own."

But Gavin wouldn't budge. Instead, he positioned himself next to me on the bed, brushed a stray strand of hair away from my eyes, wrapped his arms around me, and pulled me in closer.

"Sweetie, you deserve to get help for yourself. After what I saw a couple of months ago, you need to talk to someone."

I didn't want to hear a word he was saying. The idea of seeing a therapist terrified me, but Gavin wouldn't give up on me.

"Yvonne, something is haunting you. You scream in the middle of the night, you cry uncontrollably, and you've barely been out of this bedroom in months. It's just not healthy for you. As your husband, it's my duty to take care of you, so please let me do that."

He stood up to grab a piece of paper from the printer and held it out to me.

"Here, please take a look at this."

"What is it?" Irritated, I tore the paper from his hand.

"Please, just trust me and look."

Gavin had been insisting I go to therapy ever since that call with my mom. I gave him one last scathing look before I agreed to take the paper. When I realized it was a list of potential therapists, a deep, involuntary sigh escaped my body. I barely had the energy to sit up, but I threw my favorite purple plush blanket aside, revealing the same grey joggers and light blue tank top I'd worn for days, and quickly browsed the list.

The impending dread of starting therapy made me nauseous. Shame rushed through my body at the realization that I was not the same woman Gavin fell in love with back in October 2012. When we met, I was at the height of my sales career and dressed in designer clothes every day. My hair and makeup were on point, and you'd hardly see me without a smile on my face. I'd been divorced from my first husband, Brent, for four years and shared custody of our two daughters, Ashley and Claire.

Now, just three years into our relationship, and two months after our fairytale wedding, I'd become increasingly helpless and weak. I fell into a dark rabbit hole of deeply intrusive thoughts, flashbacks, and night terrors so vivid I'd wake myself in the middle of the night screaming and crying. At my rock bottom, I realized I couldn't claw myself back to the top alone, and Gavin came through with the support I needed. He spent hours preparing the list of therapist names, addresses, and even included their photos.

I scrolled down the list a couple of times before stopping at a photo of an attractive female therapist named Laura. She had long, blonde hair and a welcoming smile. I pointed to her picture.

"Let's try her," I mumbled. I'd never met her, but I already felt a connection.

"Are you sure?" Gavin asked.

After a brief pause, I nodded and gave Gavin the permission he'd been begging me to give. He walked back to his desk to retrieve his phone. My heart pounded as he dialed the number. He gently placed the phone on the desk and pressed the speaker button. It rang three times before the messaging system picked up.

"You've reached my confidential voicemail. Please leave a message, and I'll call you back," said a gentle voice, but I still trembled as Gavin prepared to leave a message.

"Hello, my name is Gavin, and I'm calling to make an appointment for my wife, Yvonne. Please call us back at your earliest convenience."

Gavin repeated our phone number and hung up. I let out a deep sigh, relieved that she didn't answer. I fell back onto my pillow and pulled my trusty purple blanket up to my chest; *at least I tried*. I secretly hoped she wouldn't call back. But within minutes, that hope shattered at the sound of Gavin's phone ringing.

Gavin answered quickly, mouthed to me, "It's Laura," and my heart sank. He put the phone back on the desk and put the call on speaker.

"How can I help you?" Laura asked.

"I need to make an appointment for my wife," Gavin explained.

"Can you tell me a little bit about what's going on?"

"I'm not sure. A few weeks ago, she fell into a trance, and said some disturbing things."

"What did she say?" Laura asked.

"She said she was molested, and no one protected her. She also said that someone raped her more than once as a kid. It was horrible."

"What did you do?" Laura asked.

Gavin shrugged. "I tried my best to comfort her. I just hugged her until it was over."

"Is Yvonne there now?"

"Yes, she's here. The call is on the speaker. I don't know if she will talk to you, but I'll try."

Gavin pushed the phone closer to me, pleading with his eyes. "She needs to talk to you, honey." I felt the pressure building inside my chest as I once again tossed my blanket aside and moved to sit with my legs dangling over the edge of the bed. My head fell into my hands, *Fuck! I'm not ready for this!* I took a breath and quietly spoke into the air.

"Hello."

"Hi, my name is Laura. Can you tell me what's going on?"

I looked at Gavin nervously and shrugged, *I don't even know where to begin?* "I don't know. I'm just not feeling like myself. I'm sad. I cry all the time, and I've lost all ambition. I feel overwhelmed and lost."

"I'm glad you called, Yvonne. That was very brave of you."

"I didn't even make the call," I snapped back.

"Well, you're talking to me now, and that's all that matters. I'd like to see you as soon as possible. Can you come in tomorrow at ten a.m.?"

I looked at Gavin, wanting to answer "no," but I knew he already cleared his calendar for the day. "Yes."

"Good. I'm looking forward to meeting you."

"Can I give the phone back to Gavin now?" I asked rudely.

"Yes, I'll give him the address. Thank you again. I'll see you tomorrow."

After that first call with Laura, Gavin sat next to me on the bed and took me into his arms; his broad shoulders and chest protecting me. I nuzzled my face closer to him and took a deep breath.

"I'm proud of you, sweetie," he said. "I know that wasn't easy."

"I don't want to go," I groaned.

"I know, but it's going to be good for you."

"Easier said than done. But I know I have to break down to break through, so at least I'm halfway there. I've got the breaking down part; now I need to break through."

Gavin smiled down at me and kissed my forehead. I realized I needed his permission to take this time to focus on myself and get the help I needed, but the idea of reliving my past terrified me. I already felt guilty about my depression and worried, *What if therapy makes me feel worse?* Gavin became my rock, my support system, my source of light, happiness, and comfort. He selflessly and genuinely loved me, which was something I'd never experienced. It was the first time I'd ever felt safe and secure or trusted anyone to do what was in my best interest. I wanted to give up on life, but Gavin wouldn't let me. He saw that I could no longer brush the pain aside and put on a happy face. I knew the pain was so poignant and agonizing I could no longer ignore it.

Deep down, I knew I needed support, even if I didn't want to admit it. I was not a functioning, healthy adult. I stopped showering, brushing my teeth, changing clothes, or taking care of basic needs for days at a time. I didn't drive, shop, cook, clean, keep up with laundry, or engage in ordinary, everyday activities, such as school pickups and drop-offs. I didn't leave the house unless it was a necessity.

Without skipping a beat, Gavin stepped up to take care of the girls when they were home. He helped with homework, cooked dinner, cleaned the house, and did the laundry. All while working tirelessly every day to grow his own business in the auto industry to support his family. I already knew Gavin was my soulmate, but his selfless actions proved it during these challenging times. He gave me the safe space I needed to finally deal with my painful past. At the time, it meant isolating myself in our bedroom and crying for days. Gavin never shamed me or asked me to be anyone other than myself. He encouraged me to take as much time as I needed to feel better. Neither of us knew how long it would be, but he made it known that he was in this for the long haul.

When my flashbacks were at their worst, I'd secretly hurt myself to express my pain when I couldn't find the words. I'd hide away in the bathroom to scratch my arms with my fingernails, which escalated to lying in bed and allowing my black-and-tan Pomeranian to gnaw at my hands until they numbed. Though his teeth never broke the skin, his bite was just painful enough to distract me from the emotional anguish boiling over inside me. The physical pain comforted me when floods of undesirable emotions overwhelmed me.

In the most intense moments, I lashed out violently but struggled to remember my erratic behavior. Gavin described the "incidents" to me after I calmed down. It usually involved screaming, punching, and kicking whatever solid surface was in front of me. Thankfully, I've never gotten violent with Gavin or my daughters, but the violence toward myself was equally unacceptable.

Over the next six months, I immersed further into my depression and became more out of control of my emotions. It turns out that my new relationship's stability made it safer for me to explore the remnants of my past, and my subconscious broke wide open. When it did, the pain, shame, guilt, and blame from my past traumas came rushing back and almost sent me over the edge with suicidal ideations.

Gavin was by my side every step of the way. He began encouraging me and supporting me in ways I'd never experienced before. For the first time, someone wanted to hear about my feelings. He didn't tell me to "get over" anything or downplay the significance of the emotional turmoil I was experiencing. Instead, he reassured me when I felt down, picked up the slack when I was falling behind with chores, and reminded me daily how much he loved, respected, and needed me. The difference this time was that Gavin didn't just speak the words, he followed through with meaningful action, which created the space within our relationship for me to deal with these suppressed emotions that now flowed freely. Deep, emotional pain caught up to me after years of trying to snuff out the memories. Gavin always filled in where I fell short without complaint, but I knew it was hard on him. He is my knight in shining armor. His armor is his heart, and his unconditional love for me protected me. Still—I feared the day would come when I'd be too much to manage, and he'd just leave me like everyone else did.

Let me take you back to the beginning.

Mama was born in Northwest Georgia in 1961 and grew up all over the United States while Pawpaw made his living traveling with his bluegrass band. When Mama was a teen, Pawpaw settled the family down in central Georgia, and made his living as a cemetery owner and plot salesperson. Granny stayed home to raise their four daughters and two sons. She never learned to drive or tasted a drop of alcohol. Mama was the third oldest and told me she felt like the pariah. She was a teen mom, amongst a valedictorian, musician, cheerleader, and a couple of college graduates. Mama says her childhood was great, so I'm not sure what there was to rebel against, but the truth is Mama was still a child herself when Daddy began abusing her. I realize she lacked protection from her parents, and unfortunately, that lack of protection carried over to me.

Daddy grew up in North Alabama on a vast property that overlooked hay fields, rose bushes, and grapevines. Grandpa owned a few chicken coops and worked for public transportation until the day he died. My grandma worked in the deli department at their small-town grocery store. I never had a consistent relationship with Daddy's side of the family. He was one of three children, but sadly his brother died as an infant, so it was just him and his younger sister growing up.

Mama and Daddy met in 1975 at the ages of fourteen and seventeen in Alabama before Pawpaw moved the family to Central Georgia. Mama was a beautiful and naive teenager with long, chestnut-brown hair and piercing green eyes. Daddy had curly, mahogany-brown hair, brown eyes, and a thick '70s mustache. He was the rebellious type she liked. Daddy liked to party, and Mama liked his bad-boy attitude. Daddy once told me he fell in love with Mama's long hair and green eyes. Mama said she never really loved Daddy at all. But that didn't stop them from having a child less than a year into the relationship. Even at fourteen, getting pregnant came with a price. My old-fashioned grandparents shamelessly pressured Mama to drop out of the eighth grade and marry my daddy. Mama was still a child herself, but appearances were important within their deeply religious circle of friends. My grandparents didn't want people to judge them for having a grandchild out of wedlock.

In June 1976, three months after her fifteenth birthday, Mama married Daddy at the courthouse. Mama didn't have much time to adjust to married life, because within six short months, my oldest brother, Michael, came into the world. Mama was an official teen mom, and Daddy, at eighteen, was a dangerous alcoholic. The constant drama and chaos in our household was enough to keep the property owners busy writing eviction notices. My parents already had a turbulent relationship, and over time it only got worse. Not only did Daddy's alcoholism intensify, but he began having frequent violent outbursts toward Mama.

I was born two and a half years later in the middle of a scorching Alabama summer in 1979. When the big day of my arrival came, it was just me and Mama at the hospital. Mama preferred to go through labor alone because Daddy wasn't a supportive husband. He stayed behind to take care of Michael instead. The maternity ward was much more peaceful than being home. Mama relished in the one-on-one time we shared and only put me down to sleep. Mama tells me we spent forty-eight joyful hours in the hospital until Daddy's drunken and dramatic entrance disrupted our peace and quiet. Mama recounted the moment Daddy bent down to kiss my forehead, and she detected the stench of whiskey on his breath.

"Where's Michael?" Mama asked nervously.

"With the sitter," Daddy barked.

Mama assumed Daddy spent the previous forty-eight hours taking care of his alcoholism instead of tending to his son's needs, but she kept her concerns to herself and packed up to go home. Still drunk from the night before, Daddy carelessly drove us home from the hospital. Mama knew not to argue with him.

Mama told me our white, tattered mobile home sat at the end of a long gravel driveway. Loblolly pine trees shaded the small lot and sharp pinecones covered the ground. Daddy unlocked the front door and ushered Mama inside while I was in her arms. Mama quietly stepped over trash, empty beer bottles, and pizza boxes to get to the living room sofa. The whole place looked more like a college dorm room than a family home, but Mama didn't say a word about it. She sat on the couch, holding me close to her chest, until my dad directed her to put me in my bassinet and get to work cleaning up his mess.

Mama learned the hard way not to go against his wishes. She was careful to pick her battles but still carried bumps, bruises, and black eyes several days a week from his alcohol-induced rages. Dad's anger became more unpredictable the drunker he got, and he was never without a beer in his hand. I wondered if anyone ever stepped up to help Mama until I learned that my grandparents were very aware of the abuse and did nothing to help her. The family didn't encourage her to escape; instead, they coached Mama to not upset her husband. The rules were simple. Just do what Daddy said and everything would be fine. Still, the reality was much different than the illusion of control her family tried to convince Mama she had. It gave Mama a false sense of security and a more profound sense of obligation to stay in the marriage. Domestic violence became the norm for our family, and things only got worse. My Grandma on Daddy's side disowned me when I was born fair skinned with bright blue eyes and blonde hair. She questioned my paternity because I didn't share the deep brown hair, dark eyes, and olive complexions like my brother and the rest of the grandchildren in the family.

In the meantime, Mama and Daddy worked hard at the family-owned chicken coops as chicken catchers. They both bore significant scratches on their arms from the days' work. They spent hours at the chicken farm chasing free-range chickens, catching them barehanded, and throwing them into cages. I remember the long-sleeved plaid shirts my parents wore to hide their arms. The stench from the coops stuck to their clothing like smoke and became a familiar smell to me. The white 1970s GMC Suburban my parents drove smelled worse than their clothes. They'd keep their chicken-manure-covered boots in the back. Daddy recently told me there was something special about my mama at the time.

"She outworked every man there," he boasted. I wondered where that motivation to work went when we were kids and needed it the most. I don't recall my mom having a steady job until I was a teenager.

I've felt alone my whole life, like every adult in my life let me down. My dad abandoned me when I was nine, my stepdad abandoned me when I was fourteen, and Mama let me leave home when I was fifteen. Experience taught me that people rarely stay when times get tough, so I didn't expect Gavin to be any different. At the time, I only hoped that therapy would help me find myself again before it was too late.

CHAPTER TWO:
FLASH BACKS

"Good morning. How're you feeling today?" Gavin asked the morning of my first therapy appointment.

"I'm not feeling well, my body aches all over."

"Do you remember what happened last night?"

Gavin had a concerned look on his face as he opened the blackout curtains to let in some of the morning sun. I sat up in the bed, scraping the crust from my eyes. *What did I do now?*

"No, I don't know. What did I do?"

Gavin stood in front of the dresser, picking out his outfit for the day. He tossed a T-shirt, pair of jeans, socks, and underwear onto the bed and then sat next to me, placing his hand on my thigh.

"Something triggered you hard, and you sobbed on the bathroom floor for hours. You don't remember anything?"

"No, I don't."

"Do you remember me hugging you?"

"No, I'm sorry, I don't."

"I held you tight, hoping to calm you down, but nothing worked. I guess it's a good thing you have your appointment today. Are you ready?"

"Not at all. I'm dreading it."

"I'm sorry. Hopefully, you'll feel better after. Do you want breakfast?"

"No, thanks, I'm not hungry, but coffee would be amazing."

"Coming right up."

Gavin quickly dressed, gave me a reassuring hug, and headed downstairs to the kitchen. I dropped myself back on the bed and stared at the ceiling. The thought of leaving the house felt agonizing. After a few minutes, the smell of bacon and fresh brewed coffee filled the air. I tossed my blanket off my nude body, stood up, and slowly walked to the bathroom. I spent a few moments staring into the mirror, *How did things get this bad?* My once-youthful face now appeared aged at just thirty-six; my long, auburn hair hadn't been cut in a year; and my bright blue eyes had faded. I turned on the faucet and splashed my face with cold water, hoping it would snap me out of my daze. *Maybe a shower will be good for me?* My appointment was only two hours away, and I needed to get ready. I turned the shower on and stood motionless with my hand under the falling water, waiting for it to heat up. Instead of stepping into the enclosed shower, I again fell to the stark white tile of the bathroom floor and began sobbing uncontrollably. The overwhelming sorrow I felt sent me crashing to the floor in an emotional outburst, and the only thing left to do was sob through it. A few minutes later, Gavin returned to the room and ran to my side.

"Yvonne! It's okay; I'm here with you."

I could barely speak through my tears, but I mustered the strength to try to explain what my tears were saying.

"I hurt so bad that I want to die! Please, just let me die!"

"Yvonne, you don't want to die. We need you. Your girls need you. I need you."

18

"How can you love someone like me? I don't deserve your love!"

Hysteria took over my mind and body, and I became entirely out of control. My first therapy appointment was hours away, and I just wanted to end it all. No one could understand what I'd been through as a child. I'd been walking wounded since I was three years old and somehow managed to keep my composure. The dam cradling my past emotions broke wide open, and the pain felt too much to bear. Before I knew what was happening, I stood up, wrapped myself in my tear-soaked towel, and ran out of the bathroom. Gavin followed right behind me.

"Yvonne, where are you going?"

"I'm killing myself. I can't take it anymore!" I screamed as I stormed downstairs, laser-focused on reaching the kitchen knives. I often felt like an encumbrance to everyone around me and thought they'd be better off without me. I held the irrational belief that my depression was more detrimental to my daughters than not having me around at all.

Gavin caught up to me as my hand reached the first knife handle and pulled me in close to him.

"Yvonne, you don't want to do this. I promise you."

I didn't want to hear it. It was his fault this was happening. He was the one forcing me to go to therapy. His presence suddenly infuriated me, and guilt about my past consumed me. I felt responsible for everything that happened to me as a child. I blamed myself for not leaving sooner, running away from the perpetrators, or calling the police. If I'd just done this or that back then, I wouldn't be going through this hell now.

I wiggled away from the clutch of Gavin's protective arms. I began punching the pantry door repeatedly, scraping my knuckles and leaving my hands with painful bruises that tingled for days. I finally tired myself out and fell back into a fetal position on the floor. Fortunately, the girls were with their dad and didn't see this explosive moment. I tried to be mindful of their best interests and managed to stay more present when they were with me. But with an empty house and the security of Gavin's support, my painful history finally had room to show itself.

Gavin didn't know much about my trauma at this point, but that was about to change. I heard Gavin's voice trying to console me, but the words weren't reaching me. Raw memories flooded my mind and overpowered my heart with pain. Sweeps of intrusive thoughts from my shuddersome past played in my mind like a movie montage. It was like the traumatic events were happening all over again. I felt guilty that I'd become a burden to my husband. He gave me his wholehearted support before knowing what he was getting himself into.

Allowing these aged emotions to come to the surface was torturous. It caused tormenting, vivid nightmares every night that felt so real I'd wake up with what I call a "nightmare fog." That's when the emotions from a dream bleed into waking and can be difficult to shake for hours. My secrets ran deep, and with time to finally focus on myself, things came up that I'd kept hidden for years. I kept myself distracted with work, kids, and anything else to avoid confronting inner demons from my past. Thanks to Gavin's support, I had the opportunity to take a break from work and make healing from my past my full-time job. I didn't want to go to therapy but had no other choice. I started having suicidal ideations, and for the first time, I feared that I could be a danger to myself. I felt I would've already taken my life without my daughters or Gavin to look after.

I drifted up the stairs, feeling lightheaded from my outburst. I swung the closet door open and grabbed the first schmatte hanging in front of me. I sat on the laundry-covered massage chair and pulled a pair of tan sandals over my unmanicured toes. *I don't care what I look like, I just want this over with,* I thought as Gavin returned to the bedroom, this time holding my light blue coffee thermos.

"Here's your coffee. Maybe it'll make you feel better." Gavin said with a smile.

I couldn't force a smile back this time. "Nothing seems to make me feel better these days." I took the thermos from his hand and took a sip. "But this coffee is incredible, thank you, baby."

"Are you ready?"

"Not at all."

Gavin ran his fingers through my hair, not knowing what else to say. I followed him as he bounced down the stairs toward the front door but began bawling again as we approached our navy-blue SUV and didn't stop for the entire fifteen-minute trek to Laura's office. We arrived a few minutes early, so I tried to calm down before getting out of the car. *Deep breath, Yvonne. Everything is going to be okay,* I kept repeating to myself. I looked over at Gavin and nodded, giving him the signal that I was ready to go inside. He smiled and kissed me on my cheek.

"Let's do this," he said with a grin.

During the short walk from the car to the building, my fear intensified. Even more so when I realized Laura's office was the first door on the right as soon as we entered. No elevator ride or walk down a long hallway to give me time to mentally prepare. Gavin opened the door to the waiting room and a bell jingled to announce our arrival. The sound of opera music filled the air and there were posters and pictures on every wall. I sat on a wood bench with my back to Laura's office. Gavin sat next to me and wrapped me up in his arms. As we waited, I frantically wondered, *Where should I begin? There are thousands of fragments of memories that I could talk about for days.* Before meeting Laura, I questioned her ability to help me. I tried therapy once before, but it wasn't effective. The therapist just wasn't a good fit for me. I didn't trust her to open the vault of my hidden agony, and I didn't expect this experience to be any different.

I looked over at Gavin sitting next to me and allowed myself to feel a little optimism. I told myself, *This time will be different because I have Gavin's support.* I surrendered to the process, not wanting to reject the help I'd needed for years. The thought alone left me brimming with anxiety, so I refocused my attention on the pictures hanging on the wall. I glanced at them but stopped when I came to a poster with the words of Virginia Satir's "I AM ME." The sound of peaceful classical music now filled the air as I studied the poem from start to finish. Reviewing it, I realized for the first time that I wasn't okay. I didn't own my body or my voice, I certainly wasn't being friendly and loving to myself, and at that moment, I felt hopeful that things could change.

As I took in my surroundings, I relaxed a little. The wood wicker furniture with ivory cushions felt familiar, along with the handmade dolls sitting atop shelves, but I still felt deeply uncomfortable. After a brief wait, the door opened, and my heart began racing. *Why am I here?* I thought. *I'm not ready for this.* My anxious thoughts enveloped me when the friendliest face I'd ever seen popped out of the doorway. Laura looked exactly like the photo I'd seen online, and as she introduced herself, I felt more at ease. Laura had a comforting aura about her that drew me in. It could've been the gentle tone in her voice or her flowy, long white skirt.

"Please come in." Laura welcomed us into her office with a warm smile.

The office was large enough to house an enormous bookshelf, an '90s-era pinstriped sectional sofa, and a full-size office desk. I quickly found my "spot" on the corner of the sectional, closest to Laura's desk. I sat lifeless with my head hanging and my hands in my lap. Before Laura could even speak, extreme traumatic memories began scrolling through my mind. *A family member molested me for the first time at the age of four. By the age of fourteen, nine different perpetrators had sexually molested or raped me. One hitchhiker, one gang member, my grandpa, two uncles, and four of our family "friends." Those are only the sexual crimes committed against me. I also saw brutal domestic violence, drug addiction, raging alcoholism, and suffered severe neglect from my parents.* I took a deep breath as more disturbing images flooded my mind and waited for Laura to make her first move.

22

"So, how can I help you?" Laura spoke softly and patiently waited for a response.

I remained quiet and looked over at Gavin, begging him with my eyes to answer for me, so he spoke first.

"Yvonne hasn't been doing well."

"Oh?" Laura looked at me inquisitively. "How are you feeling, Yvonne?"

I sat quietly, feeling overwhelmed with emotion as reality set in. Unable to hide the evil secrets I'd lugged around since childhood any longer.

"Abandoned," I uttered.

"How long have you been feeling this way?"

"Since birth."

"I'm sorry to hear that, Yvonne."

Laura turned her attention back to Gavin. "When did this all start?"

Gavin took a deep breath before speaking. "She's been this way for about three months."

"Do you know what triggered her current emotional state?" Laura asked.

"Well, it started with a phone call from her mom," Gavin tried to explain.

Laura turned back to me. "Yvonne, can you tell me what happened during the call?"

"My mom suggested popping tents in my backyard for family members to sleep in."

"Why would your mom want to do that?"

"Because she didn't think everyone could afford a hotel room."

"Are you planning an event?"

"We were at the time. We just got married a month ago."

"Congratulations. I want to hear more about your wedding, but first, can you tell me more about the call?"

"Mama wanted people to camp out in our yard."

Laura turned back to Gavin. "When did things take a turn?"

"Well, I remember her mom telling her that she's changed since we've been together, and that was it. Yvonne told her mom she couldn't talk anymore, hung up the phone, and then that's when it happened."

"That's when what happened?" Laura asked.

Gavin put his arm around my shoulder for extra support. "She fell into a fetal position, started pulling her hair, and talking like a young child."

Laura looked back at me. "Do you remember that happening, Yvonne?"

"Not really. I just know I went down a deep rabbit hole of painful memories."

And just like that, my healing process began. I started the conversation I'd been avoiding for years. Only a few select people knew about my past, but that was about to change. I prepared for the array of deeply intrusive questions that would undoubtedly shake me to my core. Life, in general, presented many challenges. Still, it was the calamity of my childhood that was the root of my psychological and emotional problems.

Forty-five minutes into the session, I learned about dissociation and why I didn't remember some things. Sometimes people who've experienced trauma detach from their immediate surroundings and "black out" or forget things they have said or done. This was what happened to me the night of the phone call. After about an hour, Laura gently told us that we had to wrap up for the day.

"Now what?" I asked.

Laura smiled at me. "That's up to you. This is just our opening session. Now, you decide if you want to continue. I recommend that a psychiatrist evaluate you for medication. I'd like to start with two sessions per week, but remember the healing process is a marathon, not a sprint, so I think we've done enough for today."

I felt relieved because I had nothing more to give. I'd been sobbing for an hour straight and was happy that the session was over. I knew each visit would get more challenging as I disappeared deeper into my past. However, I felt a profound sense of reassurance after our first session. Going to that first meeting felt so daunting. Not that any step of healing is easy, but the first step is always the hardest. I finally felt hopeful and believed I deserved the help, even if that meant taking a break from my sales career. Laura didn't recommend I try to manage both therapy and my job, and I agreed. Thankfully, Gavin had flexibility as a business owner and agreed to drive me to and from my appointments.

I became deeply depressed in the days following my first session, which I learned is common. The in-between-session days were the most challenging days of my adult life. I felt completely out of control. By the time I'd been married for four months, and after two months of not working, I felt useless and like a complete failure as a newlywed.

Guilt consumed me when I couldn't perform for my husband romantically or handle household chores. It caused me to isolate myself even more, and I hated that all I could muster up the energy for was to sit alone with my iPad. It became increasingly difficult to disguise my pain to outsiders, and I didn't want anyone to see it. It was the first time I couldn't smile my way out of my feelings. I didn't know what would happen next or what my next move was going to be. The dark rabbit hole of unrelenting, daily flashbacks and suicidal thoughts deepened. My inability to control any of it made matters worse.

Before my "breakdown," I used tough times to motivate me to work harder to overcome things, but this time things were different. The realization that the healing process would be the greatest challenge of my life slapped me in the face. At that time in my life, my depression had the upper hand, and I felt defeated. I waved my white flag in surrender and prayed for the pain to go away.

Unwanted triggers and intrusive thoughts kept materializing without warning and made it much harder to cope. I stockpiled my secrets and convinced myself that I'd left it all behind. Instead, I discovered that it wasn't up to me to know when it was time to heal old wounds. It was up to my rational mind, and mine broke wide open. Righteous anger boiled up from deep within my soul as I reflected on all the memories of injustice I'd faced. I'd heard so many lies and excuses. I'd heard "I'm sorry, but" and "I wish I could" more times than I cared to count, but no one really had my back. They say it takes a village to raise a child, but no one stepped up to help me, and I wondered, *Do I matter to anyone?*

The adults in my life abandoned me and mistakenly believed that I could protect myself. I suffered greatly because of that flawed belief. When you've been through what I have, you yearn to find the positive in every negative situation. I found a positive quality in the cruelest person because my parents taught me that everyone deserves forgiveness, including abusers, pedophiles, and criminals. Mama taught me, "We trust people until they give us a reason not to," instead of showing my brothers and me that trust and respect are something someone must earn.

I'm aware now, but back then, I relied on unhealthy coping mechanisms to survive some terrible moments. Driven by repetition compulsion (the urge to put yourself in dangerous situations), I was vulnerable and more susceptible to emotional triggers and self-blame. I began isolating and taking responsibility for the appalling things that happened to me. Now that I have healthy, trustworthy people in my life, I don't hide behind the same coping mechanisms. I discovered healthy ways to grapple with the realities of my secrets. Now, when recollections overwhelm me in between therapy, I talk to Gavin about it. It helps when I'm having a "why me?" day. I tend to torment myself with questions that I'll never have the answers to like, *Where were my parents? Why didn't they protect me?*

CHAPTER THREE:
DOMESTIC VIOLENCE

My earliest memory of Dad's violence comes from when I was three years old. Those large pine trees shaded our mobile home from the blazing summer heat during the day, but the branches cast scary shadows at night.

I awoke to loud crashes and Mama's screaming. My eyes fluttered as the moon shone brightly on my face through the bedroom window. My attention shifted to the sound of another thud, followed by more shouting. This time it came from Daddy.

"You're a dumb bitch!" Daddy screamed.

I crawled out of bed and opened the bedroom door. I peeked into the dark hallway, startled again by my dad's thunderous voice, his shouting easily heard through the thin, wood-paneled walls. I tiptoed slowly down the hall to investigate the excitement. As I inched closer to the commotion, Mama's screams disrupted the brief silence.

"What did I do? No, please...no!" she begged.

I approached the doorway and stood quietly in my nightgown, my curious three-year-old eyes shifting around the room, looking for clues. Daddy looked angry again, and Mama appeared frightened. They were both standing on the bed, naked. Mama planted in her defensive position, both arms up to block her face. Pieces from the seashell bedside lamp were strewn about the floor, blocking my path to enter the room. I stood speechless as Daddy thrust his fists toward Mama's face. The brunt of Dad's attack pushed Mama so hard that she fell backward, smashing into a glass picture frame of a flower arrangement that hung on the wall. As glass shattered and blood began dripping from her back, her eyes locked on mine, and she desperately pleaded with Daddy to stop.

"Stop! Eve's watching!" And just like that…it ended.

Daddy turned to see me crying in the doorway and then simply walked past me and out of the room. This horrifying scene is my first childhood memory; the image of blood dripping down Mama's back stained my mind forever. I don't remember how I felt at the time, but I imagine the incident petrified me. I didn't see love and affection between my parents, only violence. It wasn't the first time he brutally beat her, and it wouldn't be the last. Over time, many people would experience the wrath of my dad's fits of rage. The only thing that changed over the years was the severity of his abuse and the number of victims.

Back in Laura's office, I recalled the volatile atmosphere I grew up in day and night. There were constant screaming fights and broken glass around from my dad smashing things or throwing Mama into them. Mama never knew when Daddy was going to rage out. Laura clarified that witnessing domestic violence *is* a trauma for children. One of the many aftereffects from that ordeal set me up for the parent-child role reversal that began to occur.

Daddy terrified Mama, so you can imagine how I felt. He was a giant compared to me, but that didn't stop me from trying to defend Mama and Michael from his attacks. The worst beating I can recall took place when I was about five years old.

Mama took an afternoon nap while I watched cartoons from our brown couch in the living room. A while later, Daddy stumbled through the front door, still drunk from a night out partying. I watched as he staggered down the narrow hallway toward the bedroom where Mama was sleeping. I expected him to just pass out next to her, but that's not what happened at all.

"What are you doing?" Mama yelled out in bewilderment.

I ran to the bedroom to find my dad straddling Mama and punching her in the face. Mama had been sleeping peacefully, but in a matter of seconds, Daddy forced her to defend herself by violently flailing her arms and legs. Her efforts angered Daddy more. I watched in terror as he wrapped Mama's long brown hair around his hand and dragged her out of bed.

I ran toward the living room in a panic, not knowing what was going to happen next. Daddy dragged her down the hallway, her knees scraping atop the brown shag carpet as she fought to get loose. I became hysterical. I thought Daddy was going to kill her when he propped her up against the living room wood-paneled wall, straddled her body again, and proceeded to punch her face like a punching bag.

The afternoon sunburst from the kitchen bay window beamed onto Mama's face like a spotlight: left, right, left, right. It was heinous. He was relentless. Even as blood gushed from Mama's face, Daddy continued attacking her with enough force to splatter blood on the wall behind her. I jumped on Daddy's back and begged him to stop. What else could a helpless little girl do in that situation?

"DADDY! STOP! PLEASE STOP!"

Daddy shook me off his back and continued pounding on Mama's already unrecognizable face. Then, just as he'd done before, he abruptly ended his attack, casually made his way to the bedroom, and passed out for the rest of the day. The swelling from the attack scarily distorted Mama's face. I still carry that awful memory of her busted lip, ruptured nose, and painful-looking rug burns on her knees and elbows. I was just happy she'd survived.

As Mama endured more of his abuse, I became her caretaker, and she slowly forgot that it was her job to take care of me. Each

29

beating conditioned me for what would eventually become a total parent/child role reversal. I kissed her "hurts" at the age of two, which progressed into cleaning blood off her face with a washcloth. I'd comfort her by telling her, "Everything's going to be all right, Mama," even though I didn't believe it myself.

In 1986, my second brother, Christian, was born. We moved out of the Alabama mobile-home park and settled into a beautiful family neighborhood across the state line in Georgia. Oddly, both my fondest and some of my worst childhood memories exist there. I was hoping we'd have a better life and soaked in the possibilities. I was a hobbledehoy seven-year-old who loved soul music, Michael Jackson, and riding my bike. Michael was ten and fixated on Tony Hawk and skateboarding. We spent our summers riding our mongoose bikes through the woods and taking in the fresh air.

This home was a step up in status because it was our first experience living in a brick house. Sure, it was a simple, three-bedroom home with blue shutters, but to my brother and me, it was a palace. We had a carport, washer and dryer, and a fenced-in backyard with a treehouse. Being in a neighborhood with other kids was life-changing for me. We even had separate rooms for the first time. Lime-green shag carpeting covered all the floors throughout the home except for the bathroom and kitchen. Over time, I grew to hate that carpet because the bloodstains left as a permanent reminder of Daddy's frequent violence.

One day, Daddy went berserk and decimated Mama's face, leaving her in a puddle of blood in the middle of the floor. I came home from the second grade and found her lying on the living room floor. I dropped my backpack and ran to her side to comfort her. She looked up at me helplessly, and my seven-year-old self-jumped into action. I ran to the bathroom and took a white washcloth from the closet. I stood on the stepstool and wet the cloth. After wringing most of the water out, I returned to Mama and gently wiped the blood from her face, like I'd done since I was three or four. I tried to comfort her.

"It's okay, Mama. It's going to be okay," I said.

Dad's alcoholism and abuse kept getting worse. From the outside looking in, you'd never know we were fighting a war behind closed doors. Daddy worked as a successful car salesperson but couldn't keep our refrigerator and cupboards full. This is my first memory of experiencing real hunger. We survived on powdered milk, government cheese, and pinto beans but went hungry more often than not. I didn't understand how this could be since Daddy had an excellent job. No one would guess he didn't support his family or that his alcoholism came before everything else, including his hungry children. He bragged about winning sales awards and bonuses, but he was a terrible father and husband.

Daddy's abuse was a secret to everyone around us except for family. The car dealership entrusted him with brand-new demo cars, but we couldn't trust him not to abuse and neglect his family. He'd throw away empty fast-food bags at home while we were hungry and leave us home while he went out for steak dinners at night. He couldn't go a day without alcohol and became increasingly selfish with his love.

In 1989, we completed our family when Mama brought home my baby brother, York. She was still healing from giving birth and tried not to rock the boat. She quietly relied on local food banks and friends to supply food for the family when Daddy wouldn't provide for us. Mama stayed with Daddy as long as she did because she questioned her ability to take care of four children independently. Still, there were a lot of resources she could've relied on as a victim of domestic abuse. Instead, she stayed with him, keeping us all in danger.

My father had solid hands and thick fingers, but they lent no comfort. He used them as weapons too many times to be loving hands. I'd seen firsthand the damage they'd cause, and I never wanted to be on the receiving end. The final straw for Mama came when she abandoned her job at a convenience store to break up a fistfight between Daddy and my twelve-year-old brother, Michael.

Their tussle started in the bedroom and escalated quickly to the middle of the front yard for all to see.

"You better listen to me, boy!" Daddy yelled in a slurred, southern drawl.

"You don't have to hit me," Michael argued.

"It's the only way to teach you a lesson."

"I'm not gonna stand here and just let you hit me."

"Then you better get ready for a fight!"

Daddy lunged in Michael's direction and grabbed him by the collar. Michael tried to fight Dad's grip, but his strength didn't compare, and Daddy quickly overpowered him.

"Leave me alone!" Michael shouted.

Michael tore away from Dad's grip just enough to get a head start toward the front door. He thought he'd be safe if he got out of the house. I jumped on Dad's back to intervene.

"Leave him alone! Leave him alone! DADDY! STOP IT! You're hurting him!"

Daddy threw me off his back, picked me up by the neck, and pressed me against the wall.

"Stay out of this, Eve."

He dropped me, chased after Michael, and caught up with him just before he unlatched the chain to the front door and escaped. Daddy was so angry that he unlatched the door, opened it, and pushed Michael so hard he went flying out and onto the front lawn. There was fear in Michael's eyes as he gasped for air, but he refused to back down and not defend himself. He knew any attempt to run away would be futile. Daddy didn't give up on his targets.

Michael already had a badly busted lip and swollen eye from the thrusts of Dad's punches, but Daddy wouldn't let up and neither would Michael. Dad's rage ran deep. Thankfully, a neighbor called Mama at the convenience store she worked at a few blocks away. She abandoned the store and rushed home to rescue her son from his father.

I felt relieved when Mama pulled in the driveway. She broke up the fight, and I hoped this time she'd call the police and have Daddy arrested, but she didn't. Mama never reported the abuse, and it made me feel hopeless. My brothers and I received the message to stay quiet about the brutality at home. Mama threatened authorities would take us away and place us into foster care. She modeled that police were dangerous, and it was nobody's business what went on inside our house.

I ached for my brother because he had no choice but to defend himself. He knew Daddy would match him blow for blow, but Daddy wouldn't back down even if Michael cowered to him. Michael started sleeping with his shoes on, so he'd be prepared in case he needed to run. I hurt for him that he had to endure Dad's abuse, and Mama enabled that abuse every time she allowed it to go unpunished.

These distorted beliefs were why none of us had the protection we deserved. Michael and I wanted Mama to leave, but Daddy had a spell on her. I've since learned about battered wife's syndrome and how some women feel like they can't escape. Still, in Mama's case, our immediate family encouraged that distorted belief, continuing the cycle of abuse.

Mama finally left my dad in 1990 before my eleventh birthday when York was about a year old. It's the first memory I have of sleeping in a woman's shelter. I was in the fourth grade and nervous about switching schools in the middle of the school year, but I hoped Mama would leave for good. She withdrew us from school so Daddy couldn't find us. I felt petrified the first night. The shelter was just one open room with cots lined from wall to wall. Women and children lay everywhere. The room smelled strongly of body odor and cigarette smoke. I didn't like being among strangers, even though they were women. Michael and I kept a close eye on our younger brothers. After some time, Mama met a female friend named Kerri, we all moved into a small apartment together, and my brother and I registered at a new school.

We lived on our own, but the war wasn't over yet. With Daddy out of the picture, I thought Mama would become motherly and nurturing, but the opposite happened. Mama felt the taste of freedom for the first time in years and took full advantage of it. She tucked us in bed at night and then went out for the evening. She frequented a local establishment called Shakers and began meeting famous band members. At ten and thirteen years old, Mama thought Michael and I were old enough to be on our own and held us responsible for our seven- and one-year-old brothers. Mama says Kerri was always there with us, but I don't remember it that way. As a night owl, I stayed up all night watching television until I fell asleep. Some nights I'd wait all night until the channel would go off the air. I hated that time of night because it meant I'd have nothing else to distract me from the quiet nights alone. I took on more responsibility while Mama let us down and abandoned us again. Soon, she couldn't pay rent, and we received an eviction notice. Daddy rarely came around or offered financial support. When he did visit, chaos and violence usually followed, even after the divorce. Daddy pulled Mama out of multiple clubs and physically assaulted anyone she dated, even though he had a girlfriend himself.

One night he showed up to our apartment unannounced and was none too pleased to learn Mama was out for the night on a date. I don't know how he found out where she was, but he loaded all the kids into his pick-up truck with his girlfriend at the time and drove to the neighbor's apartment where Mama was sleeping over. With all of us watching, Daddy knocked and sucker-punched a man as soon as he opened the door. The two brawled on the concrete in front of the apartment before the mystery man retreated back inside and slammed the door. Daddy came back to the vehicle with scraped elbows and a bloody lip. I don't remember whether he brought us back to Mama's apartment or if we went with him. I can't make sense of the nonsense that occurred that night, but Daddy didn't come around for a while afterwards.

Neighbors and family alike seemed unbothered by the fact that children were suffering. I wondered what life would be like without my dad around. And I finally had the chance to experience a sense of peace without daily violence, sadness, and explosive anger. I fantasized that it'd be a peaceful existence, but it didn't take long for me to get a reality check. Daddy eventually disappeared into the unknown, and even though we were free from his abuse, he passed his anger onto my brothers, who physically fought all the time.

Because of my mom's financial instability, Michael and I moved to five different districts, and I attended five schools in the fifth grade. Instead of wrapping her arms around us and protecting us, Mama cut the protective cord from my brothers and me, leaving us to fend for ourselves. We were on our own, and Mama's abandonment resulted in kids taking care of kids.

On another occasion when Mama left us alone, my toddler brother, York, ran down the road wearing nothing but a diaper. I ran fast behind him, praying that a speeding car wouldn't get to him before I did. I remember hugging him tight, so thankful that nothing awful had happened to him. I placed him on my hip and carried him back home. I don't know where Mama was, but this transition became a scary time for me. Mama couldn't afford groceries, pay rent, or keep utilities turned on. At the time, I felt helpless and hopeless, but I had to pick up the pieces and keep going. I wanted to be Mama's "bright light" in the day, so I never complained or fought with her.

When Mama met a man named Mark and fell head over heels in love, we thought our lives would change forever. Mark came to the States from Germany when he was five years old and lived with his mom, Olga, whom we grew to love like a grandma. Our families grew very close, so I expected things were going to get better. Instead, it was like Mama forgot about us altogether.

Mama eventually moved us out of the apartment and into a tiny, white, single-wide mobile home off a dirt road. She struggled to keep the electricity turned on, but this place had a different problem. Cockroaches infested every room. We'd hear bugs scurrying across the walls while in bed at night, and they'd fall from the ceiling onto us while we watched TV. It became customary to have bugs crawling all around us, and Mama gave me a boy haircut when we eventually became infested with headlice ourselves. I wondered why no one came around to check on us. We didn't even hear from Daddy until he found out about Mark.

At this time, Mama worked as a bartender at night, so we spent many nights alone, and I hated it. Our family lived in filth, without electricity or food. If it weren't for the neighbor who allowed us to run an extension cord from their home to our front yard to power a television, we wouldn't have had any entertainment at all. Electricity was so scarce that I didn't relish normal childhood activities like Saturday morning cartoons. When we did have the luxury of television, the adults controlled the channels. We kept a blue couch outside to sit on while we watched. Mark visited us there but didn't sleep over. He was visiting the night Daddy, again, showed up unexpectedly and exploded to find Mark there. We were all sitting outside when Daddy barreled out of the car and landed a punch so hard on the top of Mark's head that he broke his hand. Dad's hand tripled in size from the swelling, and he left.

I didn't understand how Daddy let us stay there. He only seemed upset that Mama was moving on with her life and not concerned about the well-being of his children. Daddy didn't offer money to have our utilities turned on; he just let us sit there and suffer. I hoped Mark would step up to take care of us, but he didn't rise to the challenge either. We lived in those conditions the entire time we stayed there, which was less than three months.

The next neighborhood we lived in was equally dilapidated, and Mama started taking in stray animals. The abandoned animals came with fleas and ticks that caused more problems. Fleas covered my legs every time I walked into the house, but it didn't bother Mama. Her soft spot for animals overshadowed her responsibility to protect her kids. I didn't understand why anyone would take in an animal they couldn't take care of. Our animals didn't get proper dog food, grooming, or ever visit a veterinarian.

I hung all my stuffed animals from the ceiling to protect them from bugs. I didn't have a favorite; I just wanted to save them all. I shielded those stuffed animals better than Mama protected me, but I hoped she'd eventually get her priorities straight. I wasn't possessive of my stuffed animals or toys since I never got to keep them. We'd just pick up and go with the clothes on our back and start all over, rarely transferring belongings from place to place.

The only break I got during this time was when I visited my friend, Dee. We met on the school bus and became fast friends. Dee had vivid red hair and freckles all over and lived on a horse ranch. That was where I went when I wanted to get away from it all. Dee's home was in shambles like mine, and her family also lived with an infestation of roaches. The family didn't take care of the horses. Still, I enjoyed visiting them and riding occasionally, but that too ended a few short months later when we received another eviction notice.

The reality of our upbringing turned my stomach, but it was our way of life. As horrid as it all sounds, things for me only got worse. Traumas started piling up between the ages of ten and fourteen. Looking back, the only thing that helped me survive those years was my hope. Even though I lived a life I didn't want, I recognized I'd ultimately create a better future for myself.

Reflecting on such disturbing memories kept my anxiety through the roof, causing me to continue to self-harm by cutting and scratching myself. The scars on my arms serve as a reminder of the war I battled. Spending years trying to forget painful memories left me emotionally and mentally exhausted. No one wants to relive distressing memories or the relentless night terrors that come along with them. My memories are coarse. The details far too disgusting to describe, yet I knew I had to confront them to move forward. Still, that required me to expose decades of repressed and surreptitious memories that have echoed in my mind since childhood.

As an adolescent, I felt like a born loser. I was dirty, poor, and unkempt. I didn't have any friends, so I'd spend my weekends crashing wakes at the funeral home down the street. I became fascinated with death and went just to see the body. The most fascinating encounter was a sixteen-year-old girl who died in a car accident. She looked beautiful, lying in the white casket. She had long, blonde hair that rested on the shoulders of the lacy white dress she wore. I cried for her family and friends as I watched them grieve. It made me think about my funeral. *Would anyone care? What would they say about me? What will people remember about me?*

It reminded me of my own grief. The loss of happy childhood experiences. I've collected a few photos from different family members, and each picture is a painful reminder of how people overlooked my needs. I'm either wearing tattered, hand-me-down clothes from my brothers or clothing that didn't fit. Those photos also remind me of what was missing. There's no sixth-grade graduation photo, no first day of kindergarten photo, no first birthday memory—no birthday memories at all. I don't have a single picture to celebrate me or any childhood milestone. It's a painful realization that my parents robbed me of the parental love and support that all children need and deserve.

Growing up, the only tradition we had was Thanksgiving dinner at Granny and Pawpaw's house in Georgia every year. It was the one day I knew I'd get a good, home-cooked meal. I loved Granny's homemade buttermilk biscuits, chicken and gravy dressing, homemade pies, and the camaraderie of family.

Granny and Pawpaw built a modest, three-bedroom brick home with green shutters, a large front yard, and several white birdbaths placed throughout. The men usually went to the converted garage to play music while the kids played in the front yard. The women stayed in the kitchen, cooking and chatting. I loved that there was always music in the air and people singing. Pawpaw did most of the singing and piano playing, while Cousin Cranford picked on his acoustic guitar.

I loved being around all my cousins. At that time, there were twenty-two of us, ranging in age from two to thirteen. Thanksgiving was the only holiday that brought our entire family together each year, and it was my annual reminder that my cousins lived very different lives than we did. They were all properly groomed and dressed appropriately.

After dinner, Mama, Granny, and all my aunts sat on the front porch sipping coffee and smoking cigarettes. My favorite uncles, Marty and Lou, stayed close to the women. I loved it when they were around because they constantly cracked jokes and kept everyone laughing. After everyone tired out, we'd say our goodbyes and trek back home to wait for the next year to roll around.

*****

My hands trembled and my heart pounded as I waited for my next session with Laura to begin. I sat next to the man of my dreams and shuddered, thinking of the skeletons in my overstuffed closet. I went to the psychiatrist as Laura suggested and they diagnosed me with Complex Post Traumatic Stress Disorder (C-PTSD), severe anxiety, major depression, and panic disorder to boot.

In these first sessions, Gavin joined me to update Laura about my mood, dissociative episodes, and nightmares. I worried, *What will he think? Will his feelings for me change?* I never trusted anyone the way I believed in this man. He gave me the freedom to release the baggage I'd been carrying for thirty-six years.

"Good morning, Yvonne and Gavin. Come on in."

I took a deep breath and walked into the office without saying a word.

"How are you today?"

I shrugged and hung my head lower. Gavin broke the silence.

"It hasn't been a good couple of days for her."

"I'm sorry to hear that, Yvonne. Do you want to tell me what's been on your mind?"

I shook my head. Gavin put his arm around me and pulled me close. "Sweetie, I know this is hard for you, but it's time to let go and let Laura help you. Do you think you can do that?"

I wanted to make Gavin proud, so I agreed to talk about one of the worst memories of my life.

Laura looked at me and said, "Whenever you're ready."

The truth is, I wasn't ready. I wanted to run out of the office, but I couldn't deny the anguish that developed over the months. Something changed me, and I'd just have to deal with it. I needed to expose the people who did horrible things to me, and Laura was going to hear about every single one. I needed to illuminate everything, so I closed my eyes, took a deep breath, and began.

"At the age of four, I developed my first compulsive behavior, and I remember the exact moment it started. My dad's Uncle Trevor lived a couple of trailers behind us. One night my brother, Michael, and I spent the night with Uncle Trevor and his male roommate."

I stopped to take a break and looked up at Laura. She smiled and nodded for me to continue.

"At bedtime, Trevor tucked my brother in on the couch and then led me to his bedroom to sleep. His bedroom was small, with a twin bed nestled up against the wall. I started to climb into bed with my one-piece romper, but Trevor stopped me and tossed one of his tee shirts on the bed for me to change into 'Here, put this on,' he said."

The fear I felt as a young girl came rushing back, and it felt like it had just happened yesterday.

"I felt frightened but changed into the nightgown anyway. I climbed into bed and pulled the covers over me."

My heart was pounding, and my hands felt cold and clammy. I was thousands of miles from that trailer, but at that moment, I felt the trauma happening all over again. I recalled every movement and ache of pain. I told Laura how I woke up the next morning to a weird sensation. I described the mahogany-brown, wood-paneled walls surrounding me and the early morning sun beaming through the window above the bed. The draft drew chills to my body, but that wasn't my focus. As my eyes adjusted to the light, I felt a terrible pain in my private parts. I looked down to find my blanket removed, my nightgown up around my waist, and my uncle Trevor forcing cunnilingus onto me and his fingers inside me.

The pain was intense, and I froze in fear. I closed my eyes and pretended to sleep. It was at that moment that I began discreetly rubbing my ear. I secretly counted out the numbers, eighty, sixty, forty, twenty, one hundred in my head repeatedly until he finished.

"After Trevor had enough of me, he shook my legs to wake me, not knowing I was alert for the entire horrific ordeal. I couldn't pretend to sleep any longer. The reality of what just happened hit me, and my next goal was to escape. I blurted out the first thing my four-year-old brain could conjure up and asked for a glass of milk. I followed him to the kitchen and went back to the room with my milk. I watched as Trevor calmly walked back to the kitchen to start breakfast in the front of the trailer. I looked both ways down the hall and saw two ways to get out—the front door where Uncle Trevor was or the back door closer to me. I looked back at Trevor, and when he turned his back to me, I tiptoed to the back door, hoping he left it unlocked. I slowly turned the knob, and the door creeped opened. Without a second thought, I dropped the glass of milk and ran out the back door in a desperate attempt to reach the safety of my parents. It was wintertime, so frigid air hit my face, and pain from the gravel bit my bare feet, but that didn't stop me from running away from my assailant. Trevor heard the glass break and turned to see me running. He emerged from the front door and started chasing behind me. Terror filled my body as his hurried steps, got closer and closer. I started screaming for help, 'MAMA! MAMA! MAMA!'"

My anxiety rose as I recalled the event to Laura. It's one of the most painful betrayals of my life, and I felt myself slipping away from reality as if having an out-of-body experience. My mouth was moving, and words were coming out, but I had no control over them. My pain took control.

"I thought I'd be safe if I made it to the front door," I heard myself saying, "but when I turned the knob, it didn't open. I banged for my life. BANG! BANG! BANG! While screaming, 'MAMA! MAMA! HELP!' I knocked as hard as my little fists could, but no one answered my pleas for help."

I paused for a moment, frozen from pain as my mind went back to that day in 1983.

"I kept banging and banging, hoping the door would open, but Trevor caught up to me. I screeched loudly again as he reached the porch, tossed me over his shoulder like a sack of potatoes, and carried me back to his place. I kicked and screamed, begging him to put me down. Finally, when I'd lost all hope, I saw the front door open, and Mama peek her head out. I felt so relieved and screamed again for her help, 'HELP ME, MAMA! HELP ME!' I outstretched my arms and kicked as aggressively as my little body could, begging Mama to save me."

I stopped again. I didn't think I'd get through it. I went silent, looked at Laura, and asked, "Do I have to finish this today?"

"No, but I encourage you to finish as much as you can."

"It's just that this is the hardest part for me to tell. It has caused me the most pain."

"It's okay, Yvonne. You're safe now. It's safe to tell us what happened."

I took three long, deep breaths before continuing.

"Instead of saving me, I watched in horror as my Mama closed the door and allowed Trevor to take me back to his trailer. When we got back, he yelled at me for running away. 'Why'd you do that?' he asked. I just stood in silence, frozen with fear, terrified about what could happen next. He just turned and walked away, but after a few minutes, he called out for me to come to the bathroom. The morning overcast kept the trailer dark. I turned right down the dimly lit hallway and to the bathroom's bright light at the end of the hall. When I reached the bathroom, Trevor was sitting on the toilet with his penis in his hand. And that's all I remember," I finished.

Laura took a few deep breaths herself before speaking. "Thank you for sharing this story with me. I know how difficult it must have been for you to revisit those painful memories. It will take some time to process everything, but this is a great start. That must be terribly painful to you that your mom wasn't there to rescue you from your abuser."

"Yes, it is," I admitted.

"It's understandable that you're going through a tough time right now, Yvonne. You're showing symptoms of Complex Post-Traumatic Stress Disorder. Let me ask you, what are some things you enjoy doing?"

I explained that I loved to sing, dance, and paint, so Laura suggested that I try to paint or draw out some of the pain from my past.

I never felt the same after. I felt contaminated, impure, and I condemned myself. Recalling this memory has been one of the most painful for me. It still baffles my mind how my mother – nay – ANY mother, could ignore their child in such a desperate time of need. I was so helpless. This betrayal turned out to be one of many times that Mama didn't protect me. Over time, the notion that I had no one to trust cemented into my heart. I found ways to explain away my parents' betrayals, which usually meant blaming myself.

In the meantime, it took all my strength to keep it together. It was easier to keep my "happy face" when Ashley and Claire came home, but at thirteen and eleven, it didn't take long for them to sense that something was going on with me. On my awful days, I'd stay in my room all day and night. The girls weren't afraid to ask questions.

"What's wrong with Mom? She's been in the room all day," they'd ask Gavin.

Gavin covered my back the best he could.

"She's not feeling well," he'd tell them. And that wasn't a lie.

Laura explained how having daughters the same age as I was when I was traumatized is another trigger for unwanted memories. I'd see myself every time I looked at them, and it reminded me just how young and innocent I was when I endured such horrendous traumas. On my worst days, I depended heavily on Brent to keep them an extra night or two until I came out of my rut. I am so grateful for our strong co-parenting relationship. We divorced after seven rocky years of marriage but agreed to put aside our personal feelings (and there were a lot!) to help our daughters. I never told him much about my childhood, and he never experienced my blackout rages during our marriage. However, I told him about my recent struggles, and he was supportive, especially during the most challenging times. Brent was just a phone call away, and I appreciated and needed the added support.

At a time when I felt safest, traumas bubbled up, and my Anger Monster that had an explosive temper and a tongue that cut like a knife replaced my calm nature. Anger Monster is what I call my dissociated righteous anger from my childhood. This anger comes out when a feeling from my past triggers in the present. It can cause me to scream, curse, demean, punch walls, kick doors, and throw things without remembering the behavior, like a blackout episode. Dissociation protected me by blocking memories of my angry outbursts, but I always felt the aftermath. These brief episodes of rage are the opposite of who I am, so I felt guilty when Gavin told me about my out-of-control behavior. The monster took over and made me a completely different person. It's like I didn't know who I was anymore, and I found myself wondering, *Who is the real me?* Finding that out entailed unraveling my past. I'd have to come to terms with who I was in the past to find out who I was now and who I wanted to become.

As the weeks continued, I revealed to Laura more unthinkable things that happened to me and near me as a young child. Instead of protecting their children from danger, my parents usually put us right in the middle of it. It was as if they didn't understand how dangerous these situations were, or just didn't care. For example, my parents liked to have bonfire parties. Physically combative and belligerently drunk adults who were much too unpredictable to be around kids surrounded us.

At the age of five, I saw something so terrifying that the story still sends chills down my spine. The images of the day are so shocking that it was difficult for me to recount during therapy.

My parents invited a few of their friends over to sit around the fire, drink beer, and unwind. Earlier in the evening, I walked up behind a skittish white chow dog that belonged to one of my parents' friends. The dog turned aggressive and bit me in the face. The dog's owner wore a red bandana and grabbed the dog forcefully. He pulled out a hunting knife from his pocket and threatened to cut the dog's throat. Mama was able to talk him down, and eventually, he let the dog go. But it seemed like he was looking for a reason to slice something (or someone) open.

Later that night, this same man was sitting around the fire with others. The rowdy group was a familiar scene. My dad polished off a case of beer while the other men drank whiskey straight from the bottle. Suddenly I heard two men begin to argue.

"Who do you think you're talkin' to?" yelled the man in the red bandana who had threatened his dog earlier.

Another man wearing nothing, but cut-off jean shorts replied, "I'm talkin' to you, boy!"

"You don't wanna start with me!"

"Or what?"

"You wanna get crazy?"

My parents tried to calm the situation. "Y'all settle down now before things go too far," Mama warned.

Unfortunately for us, the liquid courage already took hold, and nothing was going to stop the craziness already in motion.

45

The dog's owner stood up and pulled the same hunting knife out of his pocket from earlier and, in his thick southern drawl, said, "You ain't nothin', buddy."

We all watched in horror as he deliberately sliced his own forehead wide open. Blood poured down his face, and he shook his head violently, like a wet dog, causing blood to splatter all over me and those sitting closest to him.

Unimpressed, the other man responded, "You think that's crazy? Watch this."

He grabbed a similar knife and brought it to his stomach and sliced it open. Blood poured down his torso as he shook his body violently, causing more blood to splatter around. Both men went to the hospital, ending the party.

CHAPTER FOUR: ABANDONMENT

In 1989, when I was ten, Mama and Mark rented a place together, and I thought life was going to be different. Mama professedly met the man of her dreams and thought our lives would change forever. She worshipped the ground he walked on, and so did I.

I tried to ignore that Mark eerily resembled my dad physically, down to the facial hair. They're both about five foot nine, with deep brown eyes, dark hair, a mustache, and stocky builds. They're both alcoholics, just on opposite ends of the spectrum. Mark was a "funny" drunk, which felt like an improvement over the "violent" drunk Daddy was. Notwithstanding the alcohol, Mark brought laughter back into our lives after so many years of violence and fear. We finally had a chance to be a "normal" family.

Mark cared about education and encouraged my brothers and me to do our best. My brother, Michael, had a tough time accepting Mark into the family. Michael had so much unresolved anger from Dad's abuse that he was overly protective of Mama and had a bad attitude. Michael did what many teenagers do with displaced anger and took it out on the new man of the house. Michael wasn't ready to give up that title even though Mama begged him to back off.

Our anticipation of a better life shattered when we moved back across state lines to Alabama and into our newly rented house. This place was a yellow house, but it was in shambles. I saw prostitutes on every corner, and gang members from nearby Baker's Village ran the neighborhood. Within weeks of our arrival, gang members were trying to recruit me, but my protector, Michael, ran them off every time. Mama finally seemed happy despite our meager living conditions. While she was preoccupied, her children weren't prioritized, and we suffered in many ways as a result. I knew our neighborhood was sketchy, but I didn't know how unsafe it was until I saw one of the prostitutes shoot a "John" in the back. It's a day I'll never forget.

I was walking home from school like any other day when I heard a woman yell, "You're going to pay me my fucking money!"

I looked behind me and saw a man in a gray suit running away from one of the prostitutes I recognized from the street corner. She had long, copper-toned hair and wore deep purple lipstick. I stopped in my tracks and watched in astonishment as she raised her arm and pulled the trigger on a handgun. The man fell forward, and I quickly ran away from the scene. I was still shaking when I got home. Thankfully, Mama was home. I found her in the bedroom getting dressed.

"Mama! You're not going to believe what just happened!"

Mama's long brown hair whipped around her face as she turned around. "What? Tell me what happened!"

"A prostitute shot a man in the back."

"What? Are you sure?" Mama asked as she buttoned her blue jeans.

"Of course, I'm sure. I watched it happen."

I followed Mama to the kitchen as she lit a cigarette.

"Did anyone see you?"

"I don't think so."

"Good. Stay away from that area just in case."

I was ten years old and feared for my life.

"What if they saw me?" I asked nervously.

"Don't worry; they didn't see you. It's going to be okay."

As I reflected on this memory in therapy, I wondered if Mama should have gotten the authorities involved. It's one of the first times I learned the distorted lesson that we should protect the perpetrator, not the victim.

Mama took in more strays and strangers alike. She never contemplated how dangerous it could be for her kids. The first stranger Mama and Mark invited to stay with us endangered us on many levels. Clarke, the hitchhiker, was one of the scariest perpetrators I've ever met. Mama and Mark met him while he panhandled at the corner store. They offered him a place to stay if he'd assist with groceries from the money he panhandled. He agreed to help and came to live with us that very same day.

After a couple of weeks, Clarke's family sent money that he used to buy a white van with a broad red stripe across the side. I thought he'd leave, but he just kept the van parked on the side of our house and slept in it at night. There was nothing special about Clarke's physique. He was tall, thin, and hippie-like with long, dark hair and a scraggly beard that stopped just above his chest. He seemed nice, but most perpetrators do until you find out who they are. I found out Clarke was a rapist when he raped me at the age of ten.

It was a hot and sunny afternoon when I heard classic rock blasting from Clarke's white-and-red van. He saw me looking out the window and motioned for me to come outside.

"Do you wanna come listen to music with me?"

"Nah, it's okay. I can hear it from here."

"Oh, come on. You can hear it better from inside."

I ignored my gut instinct and naively climbed into the back of the van. He patted the seat next to him, and I sat down.

"Do you like classic rock?"

"I like all kinds of music."

"You must be mature for your age, then."

I shrugged and continued listening.

Before the first song was over, Clarke forced himself on top of me and tried to kiss me. I wore a T-shirt and shorts with an elastic waist that Clarke quickly pulled down. He aggressively rubbed himself against me before unzipping his jeans and trying to penetrate me. My ten-year-old body was seventy-five pounds and thin as a rail. Clarke didn't care that the weight of his full-grown body hurt me. I dodged his unwanted kisses but couldn't avoid the sickening stench of cigarette smoke and beer that stuck to his beard. I thrashed my head from side to side until it angered him enough to grab my tiny face in his hands and force my head to the side. His knee parted my legs, and I felt his "weapon" on the outside of my body. I clenched my body tightly, but it wasn't enough to prevent the agonizing pain.

"OUCH! That hurts!" I screamed in anguish, but my cries didn't stop him.

"You know you want this," he breathed into my ear.

His words sickened me as pain coursed through my body. It ended with a hot liquid on my body and him retreating to the front seat while I put my clothes back on. I climbed out of the van and ran to my empty bedroom. No one was home to run to for help. It was like I was four years old all over again, except this time, the only person there was the rapist, and he was a guest at our home. I sat quietly in my bedroom, alone and petrified. Clarke disappeared the same day, but the possibility of him coming back terrified me.

I didn't tell anyone about the rape because I felt embarrassed and ashamed. I blamed myself for the assault. *I shouldn't have gone there*, I told myself. These distorted thoughts can be more harmful than the rape itself. I was young, naïve, and terrified. I needed parental supervision, but they weren't there. Mama and Mark's constant absence made them grossly unaware that pedophiles surrounded me. As a result of my mom's dereliction of duty, I endured two more sexual traumas by my eleventh birthday; each occurred in this neighborhood.

Gang members kept coming around and again approached me about enrolling in their crew when they caught me outside alone. I was sitting on the front porch steps, reading a book.

"What's your name?"

I looked up to see five teenage gang members in my front yard. "I'm Eve," I responded.

"How old are you?"

"I'm almost eleven."

"Do you want to join our posse?"

"I don't think so."

He told me the name of the gang, but I don't remember it now.

"What do ya'll do?" I asked naively.

"We protect each other," he answered.

The thought of protection sounded enticing. "How do I join?"

"Normally, you'd get beat down by our female members, but since you're only ten, we do it differently."

I stared at them blankly, knowing I didn't want the beatdown. "What's the other way?"

"You have sex with me," he responded.

That sounded worse than the beating to me, and I lost all interest.

"No, thanks. I don't wanna join." I stood up to go inside the house. I peeked out the window to see the group walking away.

The next day, I ignored them when they called out to me. Late that same night, I went to bed in the back bedroom, away from the rest of the family. Mark was drinking and being loud with his friends, playing a game of spades by the light of a propane lamp. We didn't have electricity, so I slept with the window open and placed a box fan in the window, hoping to catch a breeze.

I fell asleep as usual and awoke to a terrifying dark shadow climbing through my bedroom window. Before I could scream, his hand was over my mouth, and he ordered me "not to say a fucking word."

I recognized the voice and realized it was the gang recruiter from the day before. He forced himself onto me while saying, "You thought you could tell me no. Nobody tells me no."

The assault only lasted a few minutes, but it felt like a lifetime. Afterwards, he brandished a handgun and threatened to kill me if I told anyone what happened. I believed him and kept my mouth shut, until now. The gang continued coming around but didn't bother me again. I brushed it aside like every other trauma.

My one and only friend in this neighborhood was Shannon. We met on the school bus and our parents later became friends. Remember, Mama believed everyone deserves trust until they give a reason not to, so she entrusted her new friends to care for me when she wasn't home. Shannon lived with her mom, stepdad, and two brothers. Her mom, Gina, had shoulder-length blonde hair, blue eyes, and morbid obesity. Her nickname around the neighborhood was "Sweat Hog." Shannon's stepdad, Peter, stood at six-foot-four, but his body was scrawny. I thought he looked creepy with long, scraggly black hair and an overgrown handlebar mustache.

Not long after the gang member raped me, I stopped at Shannon's house after school. Peter answered the door wearing nothing but a pair of jeans.

"Is Shannon home?"

"Not yet, but you can wait for her if you want."

I felt that same uneasy feeling I'd had before, but I pushed past it as I walked in the front door. "He's never done anything to make me uncomfortable," I told myself.

"Is Gina here?" I asked as he closed the front door.

"Nope," he answered.

I headed for the living room sofa while Peter went to the bedroom. He called for me to come to the room before I even sat down.

"Eve, come in here."

Every ounce of my body told me not to go, but my body moved as if it had a mind of its own. When I approached the bedroom, Peter was lying on the bed and started giving me instructions. I felt apprehensive.

"Come sit next to me."

Something told me I wasn't safe, but I felt trapped and did what he said. I froze and wondered what I'd done to cause it and blamed myself for going there in the first place.

"I'm gonna tell you what to do, and you're going to do it, okay?"

"Okay."

He positioned himself in the middle of the bed, with his arms behind his head and his legs open. "First, unzip my jeans."

Like a robot, I moved further onto the bed to reach Peter's zipper. My tiny, trembling fingers struggled to grip the zipper and pull it down.

"Take it out of my pants."

Sadly, I knew what "it" was. Fear consumed my body. I feared he'd hurt me if I disobeyed, worried someone would walk in on us, and I'd get into trouble. I just wanted it to end.

"Do it like *this*," he instructed before replacing his hand with mine.

My small hand didn't reach all the way around, but he told me to "move it up and down" anyway. "Just like that, good girl."

I felt sick to my stomach and just wanted to run out of the room but was powerless to flee. Suddenly, hot goo covered my hand, and it was over.

"Go wash your hands before someone gets home," Peter ordered.

I felt a panic rush over me as I ran to the bathroom. I stared in the mirror as I washed my hands, wondering if anyone would be able to tell what just happened to me. When I came out of the washroom, Peter was standing with the front door open.

"Go home, but don't tell anybody what happened. Do you understand?"

I nodded and ran home. It was another secret stuffed deep down inside that I blamed myself for. I didn't want to lose my friend, so I went on with life, pretending like nothing ever happened with Peter. I continued visiting and sleeping over. I even went on a trip to Six Flags with them. Mama let me go because they offered to pay, and she thought she was doing a good thing for me by letting me go for the experience. She didn't know about what happened with Peter or that while we were at Six Flags, Gina and Peter had sex in front of me while I was awake. They were just a weird couple.

After our return from Six Flags, I found out that Peter wasn't the only danger lurking inside their home. Shannon's nineteen-year-old brother, Joe, almost killed me. I showered at Shannon's house when we didn't have water or electricity. One night, while I was showering, Joe barged into the bathroom and refused to leave.

"JOE! Get out of here!" I demanded.

He just laughed uncontrollably, which freaked me out more. I used the shower curtain to cover my body, but that amused him more. He closed the bathroom door.

"Now, you're stuck in here! Whatcha gonna do?" He took a couple of steps closer to me.

"NO! Leave me alone!" I screamed as I moved to the other side of the shower. I grabbed the towel hanging on the rack and covered my body. "Come on, Joe! Let me out!"

Joe opened the bathroom door. "I'm not keepin' you here. You can leave if you want."

I hopped out of the shower, but he blocked the door while trying to snatch the towel off my body. I managed to push past him and ran through the house with Joe chasing me. I was terrified. I didn't know what he planned to do to me. I ran through the living room and into the kitchen toward the safety of Shannon's bedroom. My heart pounded as I rounded the kitchen table when suddenly, I slipped and fell on the kitchen floor. I heard glass explode, and then blood gushed down my left leg. When I stood up, I looked down to see my leg covered in blood and my hip split wide open. I fell onto a drinking glass that shattered inside my body, causing a deep, gaping wound. The gash was so large that I vomited every time I looked at it.

Joe ran to get Mama, and luckily, she was home. She followed him back to the house where I was lying in a puddle of blood in a blood-soaked towel. Mama quickly shrouded the lower part of my naked body in a quilt, picked me up, and carried me to her car to rush me to the hospital. I lost a lot of blood that night and have no memory of being there. I just remember leaving with over eighty stitches on my left hip. If the broken glass had cut a major blood vessel I could've died in minutes.

The more traumas I endured, the more I tried to "toughen" up to deal with it all. This time would be no different. On our way home from the hospital, Mama and I stopped at the corner store to get me something special as a treat for getting through all the stitches.

But first, Mama had questions. "How did this happen, Eve?"

My fear of losing my friend kept me from telling her the truth. "I was playing with Shannon and fell on a hunting knife."

Mama shook her head in disbelief. "I'm just glad you're okay. I'll be right back. You wait here"

"Mama, I want to go with you. I don't know what I want."

"Are you sure you can walk?"

I nodded yes and gently made my way out of the car, wearing nothing but a hospital gown and slip-resistant socks. I don't know how I managed to walk after my injury, but looking back, I can't help but wonder why Mama would let me. I can only imagine what the store clerk thought when I limped into the store. I hobbled to the candy aisle and settled on a Skor candy bar that I eventually regretted. It was too hard for my unhealthy teeth. Healthcare was never my parents' priority. A couple of weeks after the accident with the drinking glass, Mama summoned me to the living room.

"Eve, can you come here, please?"

"Comin,' Mama." Still limping in pain, I made it to the living room.

"What's up?"

"I need to check your stitches."

"Don't they dissolve on their own?"

"They're supposed to, but the doctor said they're gonna remove any stitches that didn't dissolve yet, and since I don't have the money to bring you back to the doctor for a follow-up, I'm doing it myself."

"I'm still in a lot of pain, Mama, I don't think it's healed yet."

"I think they're ready. Come here and lay down across my lap."

"I don't want to, Mama, I don't think it's time."

"Eve, just come here so that I can get this over with."

I lay on the couch and braced myself as Mama used a lighter to heat the end of a pair of store-bought eyebrow tweezers and began to tug at a few exposed stitches.

"Ouch! Mama, that hurts!"

"I'm sorry; that one's not ready yet."

Mama continued tweezing away the stitches that were loose enough to rip from my skin. I grimaced in pain for the whole ordeal and found several small open holes on the wound that Mama said would heal on their own. I suffered silently for the next few weeks as the wounds kept sticking to my clothes. Looking back, I'm lucky I didn't get a massive infection from the unsterilized tweezers Mama used for the "procedure."

I thought our lives with Mark would be different, but nothing changed at all. Mama laughed more, but we still didn't have stability or food. No roots planted anywhere. Mama and Mark couldn't get on their feet. Mark would dumpster-dive behind fast food restaurants for food to feed the family. I preferred biscuits from a chain chicken joint because I could remove the moldy parts. Before long, another eviction notice came that forced them to find yet another place to live. I was happy to say goodbye to the neighborhood, but I didn't expect Mama to take my brothers and me back to the lion's den.

In 1991, at the age of eleven, Mama sent my brothers and me to live with our dad full-time back in North Alabama. Mama's decision bewildered me. I didn't understand how she could send us back to the war zone we escaped from a year earlier or how long she intended for us to stay there. I still don't know why she made the decision, and my therapist tries to discourage me from guessing too much. I suspected she just wanted us out of her hair for a while to spend time alone with Mark. Michael was still angry about Daddy's earlier abuse, so I worried about him a lot. He was fourteen and stubborn as ever. I feared they'd have another brawl.

To my delight, Daddy rented a charming two-bedroom house right down the street from a skating rink, but sadly, his behavior hadn't changed. He was still an angry and violent alcoholic. The house was clean, and this time, Daddy kept food in the fridge. It didn't bother me when Daddy told me he worked nights and I'd look after the boys at night. It comforted me to know Michael would have a break from him. At the time, I didn't see the big deal about being alone at night. We had a roof over our heads, food in the fridge, and cable. Even alone, we felt more stable with Daddy than we had in a year. He let me spend time at the skating rink on the weekends, but I didn't allow myself to get close to the few friends I made. I didn't know how long I'd be around.

Dad's violence ramped up soon after, and as usual, Michael was his primary target. I hated the fights and struggled to intervene but was too powerless to stop them. Michael refused to back down from a row, and Daddy escalated things further, begging him to fight.

"We're not in the neighborhood anymore, boy!" Daddy threatened, taunting my brother, knowing no one was around to run to for help. When Daddy erupted, we just had to wait for the storm to pass. He didn't show any remorse after, but it wouldn't have influenced my brother's opinion; he hated our father when he was younger, and who could blame him? Whenever things started getting out of hand, I tried to reach out for help at school. I reported the abuse and added that I cared for my brothers at night. The school filed a suspected abuse/neglect complaint against my dad. I don't know what came of that report, but Mama and Mark were back to pick us up within weeks.

I didn't know it then, but I was heading directly to another war zone.

CHAPTER FIVE:
UNFORGIVABLE BETRAYAL

In the fall of 1991, Mama and Mark moved us to a small mobile home park in mid-east Alabama. I was twelve years old. As we drove up the narrow, dirt driveway, I noticed a brick duplex off to the right. We passed an old, abandoned trailer before stopping in front of a boring, brown double-wide trailer. I noticed two other occupied single-wide trailers across from ours.

True to form, Mama and Mark quickly buddied up with the two families at the duplex. Larry, Diane, and their young son, RJ, lived in one unit, and Tim, Shirley, and their four young children lived in the other. Both families welcomed us into the fold, and Mama hastily trusted anyone who proclaimed to be a devout "Christian." Tim was one of those entrusted "Christians." He was tall, with dark hair and a beard. He wore the same type of outfit every day. A white, sleeveless—"wife beater"—tank top, long shorts, and brown leather flip flops. One afternoon, while watching the kids play in the front yard, Tim beckoned me to his apartment.

"Hey, Eve, come in here for a second."

"Why?" I asked.

"I have something to show you."

My curiosity led the way as I followed him inside their apartment. Tim locked the front door and told me to go to his bedroom. I walked toward the room and my intuition screamed for me to run, but fear froze me in place. When I entered the bedroom, Tim pointed to a video of a woman using a sex toy.

"Go ahead, get a little closer," he urged. "Does the person in the video look familiar to you?"

As I got closer to the television, I recognized the woman in the video. It was Tim's wife!

"Have you ever used a toy on yourself?" Tim asked.

Mortified, I quickly answered, "No."

"It's about to get good, so keep watching."

A few minutes later, the woman began to climax, and it looked like she urinated all over herself. Tim saw the confusion on my face and laughed as he explained, "She's a squirter," as if I knew what that meant. I wanted to leave his bedroom, but he stood in front of the door.

"I want to leave now."

"I'll let you out, but you can't tell anyone what you saw, okay?"

I agreed, and he let me leave with another secret to add to my vault. I ran away and never went back, even though he and his wife remained friends with my parents. Again, I was too embarrassed to tell Mama about the video, but what happened next was far more devious, cruel, and distressing than anything else. My parents were closest with Larry and Diane. Larry was in his mid-thirties and unattractive. He wore thick, black glasses, had curly, strawberry-blond hair, and a goatee. Diane was Native American with beautiful black, coiled hair.

Diane and Larry's work schedules overlapped, so when they offered to pay me to babysit RJ, I was happy to help. They explained they needed me to watch him every day after school until Larry got home. RJ was three and an overall cute kid. I don't know where my parents were, but instead of going home (which was practically next door) in the evenings, I started sleeping over.

I would walk RJ home from the bus stop and get him settled in at home. In the beginning, I liked being there, because I got to eat dinner while Larry helped RJ with homework and got him ready for bed. That's when Larry should have sent me home, but Larry had more sinister plans in mind. One night, after putting RJ to bed, Larry invited me to play a game of poker. At twelve, I knew how to play spades, but not poker.

"Let's play a card game," he suggested. "If you win the card game, I'll pay you extra babysitting money."

"What if I lose?" I inquired.

"The loser has to take a shot of tequila."

I didn't even know what tequila was, but he made it sound fun and innocent. When he sat the bottle down, I saw something submersed at the bottom.

"What's that at the bottom?"

"Oh that? That's the best part. It's a worm."

"A WORM?" I repeated while scrunching my face in disgust.

Larry snickered at my naivety as he told me, "The person who pours the last shot from the bottle has to eat it."

"Ewwww. I'm never eating that thing." I declared.

"We'll see." Larry smirked at me and began dealing the cards for our first game of poker.

Larry's intentions were menacing and meant to groom me for the real game he wanted to play. It became a ritual every time I babysat. The setting was always the same. We'd sit across from each other at the kitchen peninsula and Larry would deal the cards. I lost every game, and Larry delighted in watching me take shot after shot. He didn't care about the risk of alcohol poisoning; he just wanted me sloshed and incapacitated, which was easily attainable since it was my first experience with alcohol. I was his prey, and he prowled on me like the predator he was. If I left a little alcohol in the cup, he'd tip the cup up with his finger to make sure I finished every drop.

He played the same music during all our card games, and unfortunately, I still can't listen to some of Genesis's songs to this day. It always happened the same way. Larry waited for me to pass out at the counter, then he'd carry my limp body to his couch. He'd replace the music with *The Rocky Horror Picture Show* movie and watch it while violating me. His unwanted fondling would snap me out of my inebriated state, and disgust would fill my body.

Larry liked to masturbate over me and try to kiss me. I hated it. I pretended to sleep, hoping it would end quicker. Then I'd feel it. The same warm goo I felt before, but this time, it was on my twelve-year-old face. That signified the end of the nightmare for that night. These violations occurred night after night for I don't know how long.

I don't know where Mark and Mama were on these nights, but I wonder why I spent so much time away from home—stuck in a continuous loop of sexual abuse with no end in sight. I didn't exaggerate when I said pedophiles surrounded us. Larry and Diane eventually introduced my parents to their friend, Nick. He owned a local laundromat and the kids called him Grandpa Nick, so I did too, even though he didn't look like a grandpa. He was in his early fifties, had a full head of blonde hair and thick, bushy eyebrows. Nick came around often, and at the height of Larry's abuse, I asked to help at the laundromat as an excuse to get away from him.

Grandpa Nick called me his official "coin counter" when we'd empty the coin machines once a week. I thought he was wealthy because he always had money to lend to my parents and never came over without gifts for all the kids. Nick bought toys for all the kids in the neighborhood and took me on shopping sprees, so we looked forward to his visits. All the adults trusted him and so did I. That all changed the night we stopped at his place after leaving the laundromat one night. Nick pulled up to a small RV in an RV park.

"Who lives here?" I asked.

"I do. Let's go inside and relax before I bring you home."

I had that familiar sinking feeling, but I followed him inside despite the alarm bells going off in my head.

"Have a seat on the couch," he said.

I sat down while Nick grabbed a beer out of the small fridge. He popped open the can, took a big swig, and rested the can on the coffee table.

"You look stressed," he said, as he situated himself on the couch next to me. "I know how to make you feel better."

Without warning, he started massaging my shoulders, and it made my skin crawl.

"Come lie down with me for a moment. I just want to hold you."

"Only for a minute," I said. "I'm ready to go home."

I had learned that if I just did what these men wanted, they'd let me go, and that was all I wanted. Nick led me by my hand to the small bedroom in the RV. We both lay on the small bed, and he pulled me close to him in a spooning position.

"You feel amazing," he said as he started grinding his body against me.

"I don't like this, Grandpa Nick. I wanna go home." I tried bargaining with him. "I won't tell anyone if you bring me home."

I guess that's what he wanted to hear because he agreed without further discussion. But this time, I wasn't going to stay quiet. I'd grown tired of men using and abusing me. I told Mama about the encounter when I got home, out of hope she'd protect me this time.

"Mama, Grandpa Nick was inappropriate with me."

"What happened?" she asked.

"He massaged my shoulders and asked me to lie in bed with him."

At the time, I expected the news to upset her, but instead, she minimized his behavior.

"Oh, he's just an old man. He doesn't mean anything by it."

Her response didn't surprise me. Around the same age, Pawpaw touched my breasts, and I told Mama right away.

"Mama, Pawpaw touched my chest."

Her response? "He just wanted to see how you're developing, that's all."

By this age, I was accustomed to being a sexual object for older men, and Mama didn't correct that flawed notion. On another occasion, I rode with Mama out to a longtime family friend's house for a visit. His name was Wade. As soon as I stepped out of our car, with Mama right next me, he looked down at my chest and said, "Oh, somebody's got some bee stings."

"Yeah, I'm really filling up," I responded.

Instead of rebuking Wade's wildly inappropriate comment or scolding me for talking about my body to an adult man, she corrected me.

"You mean you're filling out!" she said with a laugh. Wade got a good laugh out of it too.

I felt embarrassed. *Why did I say that to him?* The bigger question was, *Why didn't Mama say anything?* No parent should allow those kinds of sexually violating comments to be spoken to their children. I already knew he was a pervert. He'd take my brothers and me on camping trips and while the boys slept, he'd violate me by rubbing himself between my thighs. *Does he think I want this?* Wade had been friends with the family for many years, so I kept what happened during our camping trips to myself. Another man's secret added to my vault.

Mama conditioned me to forgive sexual molesters but be wary of anyone who criticized our lifestyle. Mama didn't want people "all up in our business." If anyone showed concern for our wellbeing, they were just "nosy," while those who hurt and abused me deserved forgiveness. It all intertwined with distorted thinking and years of fallacy of change, the irrational belief that my parents would automatically change and make better choices. Mama didn't seem concerned that Nick, a man in his fifties, tried to seduce her twelve-year-old daughter. I again speculated that Mama didn't want to disrupt the stream of cash flowing from him. I felt expected to sweep it under the rug, because that seemed more important than my wellbeing.

I continued going to the laundromat with Nick, but thankfully, he never tried anything else again.

It's hard to describe how much I suffered during those years. The lack of concern from my parents baffled me. They expected me to be strong and "overcome" these traumas, which conditioned me to suppress my emotions for years. I made it my job to be that strong little girl everyone expected me to be. Mama said I was strong, and I didn't want to let her down. I didn't complain about their disloyalty or retaliate against them with rebellion. I was respectful, kind, and obedient. Mama had enough on her hands with my brother's rowdiness; I didn't want to add to her burdens. Still, I expected Mama to protect me from danger, but she justified it instead.

I eventually grew sick of Larry sexually violating me and found a way to finally tell Mama about his abuse. I planned to fake an appendicitis to end his sick game for good. The next time he molested me would be the last.

"OUCH! Something is wrong with my stomach," I cried.

"What's wrong?"

"I don't know; my stomach is in so much pain."

Larry began pressing on my belly, and I let out a scream.

"That hurts so much!" I said as tears streamed down my face.

Larry diagnosed me on the spot. "I think it's your appendix. We have to go to the hospital."

Larry picked me up and carried me to his car. He put me down long enough to open his back door.

"Just lay down in the back," he instructed.

I climbed in, relieved my ploy worked, and Larry shut the door. He jumped in the front seat and took off fast. As I lay in the back seat, I contemplated what to say once we got to the hospital.

The car pulled onto the main highway, and I knew I was 30 minutes from safety. After a few miles on the highway, I suddenly saw blue lights flashing behind us.

"Fuck!" Larry yelled as he slowed the car to a stop. "Don't say anything."

The officer approached the window with a flashlight.

"You're going a little fast, aren't you?"

"I'm sorry, but I'm rushing this girl to the hospital. I suspect she has appendicitis."

"License and registration, please."

"Sir, please. Can I give it to you at the hospital? I'm afraid she's in serious danger."

The officer shined the flashlight in the backseat to find me sobbing. I contemplated screaming for help, but my fear silenced me. I worried, *What if I get in trouble for faking? What if no one believed me about Larry? What if Larry got angry and brought me back to his house?*

"Okay, follow me. I'll escort you to the hospital."

My memory goes blank after that. I don't remember what happened at the hospital, nor do I recall Mama picking me up. I just remember that enough was enough, and I found the courage to tell Mama and Mark about all the times Larry assaulted me. I remember starting the conversation after we got home from the hospital. Mama still had her purse strapped across her shoulder.

"Mama, there's something I need to tell you and Mark."

"What is it?"

"Well, it's hard for me because I know he's your friend, but I can't keep it a secret anymore."

Mama came closer to me, seemingly concerned. "What's going on, doll?"

I took a deep breath, and the truth came flying out. "Larry has been molesting me ever since I started babysitting RJ."

"What? What do you mean? Mark! Come here!" Mama yelled to the next room.

Mark rushed into the room. "What's going on?"

"Eve, tell him what you just told me."

"Mama, you tell him, it's too embarrassing."

"Eve said Larry's been molesting her."

Mark's face went red, and I saw his anger for the first time. "I'm going to kill him!"

He flew out the front door and stormed over to the duplex while Mama and I chased after him.

"Mark, calm down," Mama counseled. "You don't want to do something you're going to regret."

I, for one, was happy to see him express anger over the revelation. I didn't understand why Mama wasn't just as angry. When we reached Larry's house, Mark banged on the front door while screaming for Larry to come out.

"Come out here, you son of a bitch!"

Larry appeared at the front door. "What's going on?"

Not surprisingly, Mark fell short when confronting Larry. "Is it true?" Mark asked calmly.

"Is what true?" Larry asked.

"Did you molest her?" he asked while pointing at me.

"Of course not!" Larry lied straight to their faces.

I exploded. I stepped in front of Mark and came face to face with my abuser. I stuck my finger out and vehemently spoke truth to power. "You did it! You know you did it! And you're going to admit it!" I felt invincible. "You're a sick motherfucker, and I demand you confess."

I know those are strong words for a twelve-year-old, but it's exactly what I said.

I followed that up with, "You're going to pay for what you did to me. This time I'm calling the police!" And I followed through with the threat.

Police officers showed up and took Larry into custody. Mama brought me to the police station, and we filled out an official report. I recounted, on video, everything that evil man did to me. I don't remember how long the interview lasted, but I left feeling satisfied. I spoke out, and someone did something about it, which meant he'd get the justice he deserved for his crimes.

The satisfying feeling of justice disappeared when Diane bailed him out a few hours later. He returned home the same night, and I didn't want to see his face.

Soon after his release, Larry approached Mama and Mark about mending fences. He convinced them both that our families needed each other, and we're stronger together. To my dismay, my parents agreed, the charges were dropped, and their friendship resumed. I felt hurt and betrayed by my parents. *How could they forgive someone for molesting their child?*

It's incomprehensible to me how my parents could forgive him. Their treachery enraged me, though I couldn't express it at the time. The notion that my parents didn't whisk me far away from my sexual predator desecrated my hope that I'd ever receive justice for what these awful people had done to me. I stuffed my acrimony further down to be the best little girl I could be.

The lack of concern for my abuse conditioned me to accept seeing Larry around because it became painfully clear that he wasn't going anywhere. What an unforgivable betrayal. *How could my mother look me in the eye, knowing she forgave the man who repeatedly sexually abused me?* My parents expected me to forgive Larry for what he did if I wanted to have peace. I hurt deep down inside but convinced myself that if I didn't forgive him, I'd be a burden, so I let the abuse go.

Truthfully, I didn't let anything "go."

After everything happened with Larry in 1991-1992, Mama said I needed a break after my thirteenth birthday. She arranged for me to spend some time in the mountains with Uncle Lou and Aunt Wendy. I looked forward to spending time with them. They lived in a stilted house with brown wood siding in the mountains. The scenery was beautiful. I don't recall much about how we spent our days, but Uncle Lou was always on his tractor, and Aunt Wendy stayed in the kitchen. Uncle Lou was one of my favorite people. I enjoyed his sense of humor and the fact that he didn't seem to judge my family the way other family members did. He made me feel safe and accepted.

I don't know what it is about men and alcohol, but they think they can use the "I was drunk" excuse for everything, including my cherished Uncle Lou. It was a night like any other; all of us piled up in the living room to watch movies. Aunt Wendy went to bed early while I stayed up with Uncle Lou. I eventually fell asleep on the couch, feeling safe. Later in the night, Lou destroyed my sense of peace. I awoke to find him forcing cunnilingus onto me. Mortified and frozen from fear, I wanted to scream and kick and run, but fear paralyzed me again. My mind drifted off to another place while waiting for him to finish. *This abuse can't be happening to me again.* I was devastated that one of my favorite uncles betrayed me, and I knew things would never be the same.

The following morning, I woke up enraged. Whatever fear came over me the night before transformed into a fit of anger I'd never expressed before; previously, I remained silent, but this time, things went differently. I went to Aunt Wendy the very next morning and told her what Uncle Lou did to me. Aunt Wendy bolted out the kitchen door, heading for Uncle Lou sitting on the tractor. I followed behind her, ready to back her up.

"Is it true?" Aunt Wendy yelled.

"Is what true?" Uncle Lou replied.

"Did you do what Eve said you did?"

"I didn't do shit to Eve."

I stepped out from behind Aunt Wendy and yelled back, "You know what you did to me!"

"Ah, hell, I was drunk last night. There's no telling what I did," he replied.

It was happening again. Another sexual predator denies what they did to me. *What if Aunt Wendy doesn't believe me?* I worried.

"You're full of shit, Lou. And you know it," replied Wendy as she grabbed my hand. "Come on, Eve, let's go in the house."

We walked back to the house, and Aunt Wendy sat me down at the kitchen table.

"I think it's best if you go back home now," she said. "It's safer that way."

"He did what I said he did," I mumbled with my head down.

I felt ashamed, like it was my fault because she was sending me away. Now, I know she was protecting me.

"I know he did, Eve. I believe you," she said as she gave me a comforting hug.

Aunt Wendy divorced him soon after.

Before long, I was back with Mama, Mark, and my brothers. I told Mama what happened, but she didn't react much. I remember her saying, "Sometimes people do stupid things when they're drinking," which is what she'd say after Daddy gave her a beating. Mama and other family members seemed desensitized to the significance of my traumas, and it made me feel worthless and almost deserving of what was happening to me. As a child, I believed my purpose on Earth was to satisfy everyone around me, including perverted adult men.

The pain from repeated familial betrayals weighed heavily on me. It's difficult to describe my feelings after enduring so much trauma and betrayal in such a brief period. In the moment, I didn't "feel" anything at all. I mastered the unhealthy coping mechanism, "numbing myself out." I'd dissociate to detach or disconnect from feelings related to a situation at an incredibly early age. However, the "normal" emotional aftereffects of these traumas eventually boiled to the surface years later when I least expected it.

CHAPTER SIX:
MY ESCAPE

About five years into their relationship, Mama and Mark unexpectedly announced they were getting married. The news elated both families. Mama bought a lovely, white dress suit for the occasion and asked me to be her bridesmaid. I was fourteen years old and wore a peach prom dress. I stood beside Mama in the spring of 1994 as she married the love of her life in my grandparents' front yard. After the nuptials, we moved to a new mobile home situated far away from the road in mid-east Alabama, and it was my favorite place we ever lived. We had a huge front deck and the yard offered plenty of space for all of us to enjoy, including our new Chow dog we named Nakita, and I'd again have a room of my own.

Before we moved to our newest abode, I don't know what Mark did during the day. He didn't step up to take care of us the way I thought he would. He struggled to keep steady employment for whatever reason. Mama and Mark borrowed money from anyone who would give it to them. I never got the "you have to work for what you get" lectures; instead, their actions taught me that, "you get what people are willing to give." I didn't learn to have pride in our home or belongings, because we always left with less personal property than we came with as we bounced from place to place. I don't know how many storage facilities we rented, but we lost everything.

My parents put others' needs before their children by lending money to strangers, even if it left the family with nothing. Here, again, are the constant mixed messages of Mama's behavior not matching her words. It confused my self-perception. It was hard to trust how I was feeling and made me question my intuition. She taught me that's what "good" people do. I didn't have boundaries or know a friend from a foe because of this flawed belief. I hoped for real change now that we were in mid-east Alabama.

The summer of the same year felt like the start of a new life. Mark found a great full-time job and assured us we weren't moving for a long time. As a fourteen-year-old going into my first year of high school, I looked forward to staying in one place for a change.

Mark loved to barbeque and always had friends over. Michael and I learned how to play spades at an early age, so by this time, we sat around the table playing partner spades and smoking cigarettes with the adults. The adults took breaks between games to smoke pot in the bedroom or sit on the porch and drink beer.

Mark met a new drinking friend at the job named Frank. He was the same age and again looked a lot like my dad and Mark. He was taller but had the same dark eyes, hair, and mustache. Frank flirted with me, even around Mark, so I ignored the red flag. My parents were around, so I felt safer. During our BBQs, he began leaving the adults to find me inside the house. I was in my bedroom reading and listening to music.

"Whatcha doin' in here?" he'd say.

"Just reading. What are *you* doin'?"

"Nothing, I just wanted to see you."

Then he'd walk out.

You must understand this didn't happen all at once. It happened after weeks of Frank grooming me to trust him. Over time, he began staying longer and made his way into my bedroom and onto my bed. I don't remember how it started or what was said, I just remember him taking his penis out and telling me he wanted to secretly teach me how to perform fellatio on him while Mama and Mark talked and laughed on the front porch.

My entire life consisted of controlling men and their demands on me, and I couldn't escape. I was sure Larry would be the last man to ever abuse me, but I made a mistake. After Frank finished with me, he'd go back to my parents as if nothing happened. I blamed myself. *Why didn't I scream?* I became so numb to it that I just did what he said. And like many others who abused me, Frank left that day only to return weekend after weekend. Meanwhile, other unsettling life events began popping up out of nowhere.

One or two months into the marriage, Mark received sad news that his Oma died. Family needed him in Germany to help with the funeral arrangements, so he packed up without a beat. Mama understood but counted down the days for his return. The whole family missed him and couldn't wait for him to get back, but no one more than Mama. Mama imprinted Mark on her heart and soul, and things didn't seem right without him there.

Mark returned home after two long months. We were happy to have him home but soon noticed a change in his demeanor. He transformed into someone I didn't recognize. I no longer knew what to expect from him. Hwe began complaining a lot about his marriage with Mama and just seemed unhappy. Mama sensed the change too, and it put her on edge. They'd only been married about four months, and they were fighting nonstop. For the first time, Mark mentioned divorce during an argument.

"I'm not cheatin' on you!" Mark screamed.

"Then why are you hidin' letters from me?" Mama fired back.

"What letters? You're a stupid bitch!"

"Who is she, Mark?" Mama begged for the truth.

"There *is* no one else; why can't you get that through your thick skull?"

"You've been different since you've been home. I know you're keepin' somethin' from me!"

"That's it! I'm sick of this! I want a divorce," Mark screamed.

My brothers and I overheard their fight from the living room. *Divorce?* They'd only been married for four months. My siblings and I felt blindsided and hoped this would blow over. We were finally a happy family, and now he was talking divorce? It turns out that Mama had proof Mark was unfaithful while in Germany. I spent the next two months walking on eggshells.

Christmas was right around the corner, but the Christmas spirit wasn't in our house. It'd been years since we had a good Christmas with a decorated tree and gifts underneath. When I woke up Christmas morning, I was surprised to find Mama and Mark giggling at the kitchen table as they sipped their morning coffee. They seemed in a better place. I didn't think much of it after that. Mama put on Christmas music, and we ran to the tree to open our gifts. We spent the rest of the day together as a family.

The following morning, December 26th, started as a typical day. We went about our business as usual, taking a break to play cards throughout the day. As darkness descended, Mark announced to the family that he was taking his bicycle to the store to get cigarettes and would be back soon. It was only a 15-minute roundtrip ride. An hour passed, then two. Mama panicked and frantically went into catastrophe mode. Was he hit by a car? Is he okay? You can imagine the horrible things going through our heads. We depended on Mark and trusted him. He always came back when he said he would. Something was wrong. It took two full days for Mama to find out that Mark was alive and well. She showed up at his employer and confronted him during his lunch break. His response blindsided Mama.

"Mark, where have you been?"

74

"Are you stupid? Don't you get that I left you?"

"What do you mean? We've only been married for six months."

"I can't take your accusations anymore."

"It's not just an accusation if it's true, Mark. You're doin' what you said you wouldn't do. You're leavin' the entire family."

"I'm not leavin' the family, just you." Mark's demeanor remained cruel and heartless. "I can't be with you. You've dragged me down to the dumps, and I won't live that way anymore."

I found this incredibly selfish. He didn't have a problem staying with us when he was penniless. He didn't mind using our food stamps, and now that he was making eighteen dollars an hour and finally able to bring the family out of poverty, he took the money and ran. It shattered our family and any sense of security.

I later found out that Mama intercepted a letter from a woman shortly after Mark's return from Germany and learned that not only did he have an affair while he was there, but he fathered a child. Mark and his mistress hatched a plan to be together before Mark even got back. He abandoned our family to be with her. That bombshell news was more than Mama could take. She wanted to be the one to give Mark a child. She miscarried a year earlier and never got pregnant again. His betrayal sent her to rock bottom. Why would he wait so many years to marry her and then want a divorce only six months later? To add insult to injury, he stopped paying rent, utilities, and offered us no financial support. Mama was on her own again to find a place for herself and her four children. Michael was seventeen, I was fourteen, Christian was nine, and York was five years old.

Mama found work at a small motel, but she didn't make enough to take care of a family of five on her own. About a month later, the electric company shut off our electricity, forcing us to bathe and wash our hair with freezing water poured from a large cooking pot. By this time, anything left in the fridge had spoiled, and we grew hungry. Soon, the property owner knocked on the door with an eviction notice. Mama begged him to be flexible with her, but he insisted that we leave. We later learned that Mark wanted us out so he could come back and live there. He tossed us out like trash.

I asked Mama, "How could Mark do this to us? What did he expect us to do?" We needed him, and he abandoned us, ripping away the only stability we had. As a family, we lived in shambles, and the situation forced us even deeper into poverty.

The only place we had to go turned out to be an abandoned mobile home. We had no running water, which meant we went to the bathroom in buckets left outside the house. The stench in the air always reminded me of how low we'd fallen. We had visitors, which still baffles me to this day. Why didn't they help? People, including my sexual offender, Larry, came to hang out and smoke pot and then left, knowing small children were suffering. Larry continued to harass me with sexually violating comments about my body every chance he got. I hated him and hated that Mama welcomed him to our house. The last time I saw him face to face, he slapped me on the ass when I walked by him, and I punched him in the face to let him know he no longer had control over my body.

"Don't ever touch me again!" I yelled.

He chuckled, and I flipped him off as I walked out the front door to meet up with my friends, wondering why Mama allowed him to be there at all.

Mama continued working at the motel, and we eventually moved out of the abandoned trailer and into one of the rooms. She negotiated to have the cost of the room deducted from her paycheck. She worked all hours and did anything the owners wanted, even beyond her job description. The owners took advantage of her, but Mama allowed it. She merely tried to survive.

My brothers and I didn't mind the new arrangement because the pool sat right outside our door. We survived on vending machine food and anything we could heat in the small microwave in our room. Mama never kept reliable transportation, so my brothers and I missed a lot of school. We spent school hours in the motel room or swimming pool. I don't remember how long we stayed there, but it seemed like a lifetime. We didn't have visitors, but at least it was a roof over our heads. I wondered why our grandparents didn't check on us more often or why no one questioned our living conditions.

Since education fell last on Mama's priority list, I accepted that I'd never graduate from an Ivy League college. When Mama began campaigning for me to drop out of high school during my freshman year, I turned to my favorite English teacher, Stacey Lamb. Naturally, she tried to convince me to change my mind. She even had a meeting with Mama and seeing me light up a cigarette in front of Mama appalled her. She offered me the opportunity to move in with her to finish school. The idea excited me, but it never happened. Mama wouldn't have that and withdrew me from school shortly after. I lost touch with Ms. Lamb. I often think of her and wonder how she's doing. I'd love the opportunity to thank her for caring about me enough to try to protect me. It's because of her that I've had such a high regard for teachers my entire life. My thirst for learning never went away, and my curiosity about the world has grown stronger the older I've become. I've learned that knowledge is priceless; I can gain insight anywhere, take it with me wherever I go, and no one can ever take it away from me.

I turned fifteen in July 1994 and made my move away from home. I answered a classified ad to travel and sell magazines door to door. The announcement sounded enticing: "Travel the US while getting paid." It was the opportunity I'd been hoping to find. I showed up at the motel as instructed and met a man named Keith. He ran the company along with a few other crew managers. Tall, handsome, and friendly, Keith quickly convinced me to join the team. The fact that my age didn't concern them raised the first red flag. No one asked for photo identification or proof of anything. The only prerequisite was that I could travel freely. The company would take care of lodging and transportation while I'd earn a percentage of my sales and a daily food allowance. If I wanted to join the team, I'd come back the next morning with my bags packed, ready to go.

I thought it was an opportunity to see the country and make a little money in the process. I didn't look forward to breaking the news to Mama, but I knew she'd let me go. She rarely questioned my decisions. I told her the news as soon as I got home. she was in the kitchen with her sleeves rolled up, washing a sink full of dishes.

"Hey, Mama, how was your day?"

"Okay, how was yours?"

"Well, I got a job today, so it's awesome!"

Mama turned the faucet off and hugged me. "Great! What will you be doin'?"

"I'll be travelin' with a crew selling magazines."

"Travelin'?"

"Yes, that's the best part, I get to travel around the U.S., but the sad news is I have to leave tomorrow morning."

Her response was as casual as her parenting style. "Tomorrow? Wow, okay. Well, I trust your decision. Get packed up, and I'll bring you to the hotel in the mornin'."

Mama lit up a cigarette and followed me down the narrow hallway to my room. She gave me her small, blue suitcase, and I filled it with as much as I could. A few T-shirts, a pair of jeans, a pair of shorts, sneakers, and under clothing.

Mama drove me to the hotel the next morning as she promised, though she didn't bother introducing herself to anyone. She just gave me a big hug and kiss.

"Be careful out there, Eve. Take care of you."

"Thanks, Mama; I'll stay connected. Take care of you."

She got back in her sputtering car and waved her arm out the window as she drove away, yelling "Ninety-first Psalm," which is a prayer for protection. She left feeling like a successful mother because her fifteen-year-old daughter could survive on her own. In retrospect, she wasn't any different than she was when I was a younger child. I didn't have a curfew, nor was I watched over. The harsh reality is that my mom was a terrible mother. She didn't protect me from perpetrators or take care of my basic needs, but at the time, I didn't see that. A new adventure was right in front of me to steal my focus away. I wanted to meet new people, but most of all, I got my ticket out of Hellhole, North Alabama. It was my bus away from hunger, sexual violation, and poverty.

The crew of twenty or so, mostly teenagers, greeted me warmly. I imagined most of them were looking for a way out, just like me. I learned the dynamics of the group quickly. Some couples started together, while others coupled up while on the road, but no one showed loyalty to their partners. Within days, I had men pursuing me. Most were in relationships, but only one of them caught my eye. Justin looked much older and turned out to be a decade my senior. His piercing blue eyes, beautiful smile, and tattoos turned my head. He instantly fascinated me. Justin didn't hide his attraction to me, even though the crew rumored that he already had a girlfriend named Angela. It upset her when he ended it, and she became difficult to be around. She couldn't manage the breakup and eventually left the crew. I felt smitten with Justin right away and didn't care that I was fifteen and he was twenty-five. The age difference didn't bother Justin either.

I suspected fraud within the company after they failed to pay me after a month. The leading crew manager became irate when I asked about it.

"Why didn't I receive a paycheck this week?"

"You haven't made enough even to cover your hotel stay!"

That's when I learned that the company didn't pay for lodging or supply food per diem. They deducted these things from what was supposed to be my pay. I've never been one to back down, and this time would be no different.

"This isn't what I agreed to. This whole thing is a fraud, isn't it?" Keith remained silent.

"If you don't pay me what you owe me this week, I'm going to report you to the labor board," I threatened before storming out of the room. Even though it was an empty threat, I felt empowered, but within 24 hours, I was back to rock bottom.

Morning came, and the crew loaded up in the van to head out for another long day of canvassing. Every time the van stopped at a different place, Keith would call out the people assigned to canvass that neighborhood.

"Eve and Justin, this is your spot. The meeting time is five o'clock."

It surprised me because couples didn't usually get to canvass together. No one questioned it when we got out of the van, so neither did we. Justin and I spent the day going door to door, convincing people to buy magazines to pay for a college fund or anything else Keith told us to say. Sometimes it would be a college fund; other times, we'd say we worked for different charities. I should have known it was a fraud from the start. Crew managers coached us to push for cash sales although I don't know if anyone ever received their magazine subscriptions. After eight hours of canvassing, Justin and I made it back to our designated pickup spot. Five o'clock rolled around, then 6:00, 7:00, and 8:00. This was back before everyone had a cell phone, so we found a payphone to call the hotel. We thought that the van broke down or we misunderstood the pickup instructions. Instead, we found out the crew had no intention of coming back for us.

There we were, in Somewhere, Mississippi, without a place to stay. Whatever belongings we had left were with the team. Fortunately, we had a good sales day and could use that money to get us out of there. It's the only time I ever stole from anyone.

"I can't believe they stranded us out here," I said.

"It doesn't surprise me at all," Justin replied.

"Why not?"

"Because I've seen them do this to someone else. It's the company's way of firing people. They just drop you off and leave you there."

"Where can we go?" I looked to Justin for direction.

"I don't have anyone to call. No one in my family will help."

I wanted to pry, but it wasn't the right time.

"We can go to Alabama," I suggested.

"Where will we live?"

"We can stay with my mom."

"She will allow that?"

"I think she will. Let me give her a call." The call went exactly as I predicted.

"Hi, Mom, how are you?"

"I'm great, doll, how are you? I miss you."

"I miss you, too, and I have some good news."

"Oh? What is it?"

"Well, I'm comin' home."

"That is good news," Mama said excitedly.

"There's just one catch," I warned.

"What's that?"

"I'm comin' home; I'm just not comin' home alone. I'll be with my boyfriend, Justin. He wants to move to Alabama with me. Can he stay with us?"

Again, she responded as I expected. "Sure, no problem. I trust your judgment."

Mama knew nothing about this strange man that I'd only known for a month. At fifteen, I thought nothing of the age difference, and apparently neither did Mama. She welcomed this stranger into our home like a long-lost friend. In retrospect, I realize that Justin was nothing more than a sexual predator that preyed on me, and I fell in love with him.

It didn't take long for Justin to show his true colors. He shifted from a shy, soft-spoken loner to a man full of anger and disdain for women. It started with relentless emotional and psychological abuse. We'd fall asleep after chatting or being intimate, and then the next morning, he would wake up angry and give me the silent treatment, refusing to speak a word, even to explain what made him mad in the first place. This launch of psychological warfare happened more often. Justin was only interested in having sex with me. He'd go weeks without speaking to me and then demand sex unexpectedly. Desperate for his love and affection, I gave him all of me, never telling him no, but he continued to torture me with his silence. He wouldn't look at me or be in the same room as me. If I walked in, he'd leave, and it almost drove me insane. I felt so confused by how he treated me. I sensed that wasn't how love was supposed to be, but I stayed with him because I wanted to change his heart. I'd be so upset at times that I'd repeatedly bang my head against the bedroom wall. I didn't understand why he punished me, and Justin offered no explanation. Eventually, the mental and emotional warfare turned into physical violence.

I didn't understand how Mama could allow him to treat me this way. I thought she'd draw the line at physical abuse, even though she didn't do that when it was happening to her. Instead, Mama tried to "comfort" me after our fights. She liked Justin and minimized the way he treated me. Instead of condemning Justin for his behavior, she made excuses for it.

"Why is he doing this to me, Mama?"

"Well, what did you do to upset him, doll?"

"I didn't do anything, Mama. Nothin'!"

"Men do this sometimes. He just needs some space."

"But that's what I don't understand. Space from what? He hasn't spoken to me in weeks."

"He'll make his way back to lovin' you, just don't argue with'em," Mama coached.

Instead of confronting Justin for how he treated me, Mama seemed to be treating him kindly, which upset me. But, just like Mama said, after a few weeks, he'd be kind to me again for a while, and then it would start all over again. Weeks of silent treatment eventually evolved into Justin disappearing for days without explanation. He'd storm out, and I'd never know when he'd be back. Every time he left, I felt paralyzed, refusing to leave the house out of fear that I'd miss him when he came back. Sometimes, I'd wait a day or two, but he'd always come home by the third night; until the one time he didn't.

CHAPTER SEVEN:
MENTAL ABUSE

About a year into the relationship with Justin, Mama announced we were all moving to to be closer to my dad. The news shocked me, but I trusted Mama knew what she was doing, even though I had no reason to believe that at all. Mama assured us that she wouldn't reconcile with our dad; she just needed his help. Daddy hadn't sent a dime of child support since their divorce, and Mama thought he might help more if we lived closer. I didn't like the idea but had no choice.

All we could see were empty fields for miles. As with most of our moves, we didn't come with a packed moving truck, just whatever we could fit into our decrepit car and the clothes on our backs. We arrived at the new location with the setting sun. It was another trailer park. We didn't have electricity, so we had limited time to get inside to check out our new living quarters before blackness descended on the countryside. I didn't know darkness until I spent a night in the country.

Even though Daddy only lived a few trailers down from us, I avoided him. He still drank all the time and had an out-of-control temper. Mama tried her best to keep her distance too. I didn't want him to meet Justin because I didn't trust him to act like a civil human being. I feared Daddy would make things worse for me. Justin had a short fuse of his own; I didn't need my dad provoking anything.

We'd only been in our new place for a few days when Justin exploded over who knows what and stormed out the front door. He left around noon and hadn't returned by nightfall. I hoped he'd be back before anyone discovered what was going on.

"Where's Justin?" Mama asked.

"I don't know, Mama. I'm nervous."

"What are you nervous about?"

"I don't know. I just hate it when he's mad at me. I just wanna make it better."

Mama offered to get me out of the trailer. "Do you wanna come to the neighbor's house with me?"

"No, I can't leave. Justin might come back, and I need to be here."

"Okay, well, you know where I am if you need me," Mama said before closing the door behind her.

I spent the first night alone and in the dark, frantically begging the universe to send Justin back to me. The emotional pain felt familiar, but the pain that ensued the second night was something altogether different. No one came home the night before, so I lay on the floor alone and in hysterics. I started having intense stomach pain, and then I started hemorrhaging. The intense pain was relentless and made it difficult to walk, so I slowly crawled to the bathroom, turned the shower on, took my clothes off, crawled into the tub, and lay there, letting cold water wash over my body. I watched as blood flowed from my body and down the drain. I closed my eyes, hoping I'd fall asleep and wake up to a different reality, but the pain kept me from sleeping. Instead, I let the water wash over me for what seemed like hours.

After two days, the physical pain subsided, leaving room for the emotional distress to come back to the surface. Even though the

86

pain was agonizing, I never went to the doctor about it. I just thought the stress-filled affliction of Justin leaving caused the pain. I didn't consider that it could've been a miscarriage until a few years ago. The most challenging day came on day three. Justin usually came back by this time, but things felt different. Mama came home to find me in the bedroom, still crying uncontrollably and asking why Justin did this to me. Mama tried to console me, and we both jumped when we heard someone knock. I barreled to the front, hoping to see Justin standing on the other side. Instead, it was a neighbor with a message from Justin.

"Justin called and asked me to get a message to you."

"Where is he? Is he okay?"

"He's fine. He's in Florida."

"Florida? How did he get to Florida?"

"He hitchhiked."

"What's the message?"

"Justin said you have three days to get to Florida, or he's gonna kill himself."

I never expected to hear that he hitchhiked to Florida of all places. Questions started flying through my mind. *How did he contact the neighbor? Why would he go to Florida?* Panic-stricken, I desperately started thinking about ways to get to him.

"How does he expect me to get to Florida?" I asked.

"I don't know; I'm just giving you the message."

After the neighbor left, tears flowed down my cheeks. I didn't have money for lunch, let alone a ticket to Florida, but Mama gave me an idea. "Why don't you go door to door asking the neighbors for money for a bus ticket?"

A Greyhound ticket to Florida was $79.00, and I did not think I'd be able to do it. We'd only been there a few days, so the neighbors were strangers to me, but I tried it and to my surprise, I scraped together the money and got ready to go to the bus station. Again, Mama aided in my "great escape" by giving me a ride. She did not wait at the station with me; she just dropped me off.

"Come give me a hug," she said as she wrapped her arms around me. "I hope things are better for you in Florida."

"Me too, Mama. Hopefully, we'll be happier there."

"Take care of you, doll."

"Take care of you, Mama."

"I love you. Ninety-first Psalms," Mama whispered in my ear.

"I love you too, Mama."

Neither of us had a reason to believe anything would be better, but I remained hopeful. I had plenty of time to reflect during the three-day bus ride. I had no idea what awaited me there, but as a sixteen-year-old kid with nothing to my name but a bag full of clothes and blind faith, I welcomed the new adventure. Justin rarely spoke of his family, so this territory was unknown. I'd meet his mom, dad, and two of his sisters right away. The only thing I knew about his mother was that Justin hated her and wanted nothing to do with her. I called Justin when I reached Florida and learned that, surprisingly, he sent his mother to pick me up. I hoped Justin would surprise me and come with her, but she arrived alone. He waited for me back at the apartment.

Justin's mom wore tortoiseshell eyeglasses and was petite with short blonde hair. She proved to be a quiet woman and was visibly uncomfortable in my company. It's like she wanted to know nothing about me. She only spoke long enough to inform me of a few things.

"This is me," she said, pointing to a beige minivan.

"I appreciate you picking me up."

"You're welcome, but you won't be staying at my house," she said as she opened the hatch.

I didn't care where I slept if I'd be with Justin.

"How's Justin doing?" I asked as the hatch closed.

"He's okay, I guess."

I didn't know his state of mind since he threatened suicide a couple of days earlier. After a short ride, we pulled into a small apartment complex. I recognized Justin waiting for me in the doorway, and I felt relief. Soon, that relief was replaced with awkwardness and tension so thick you could cut it with a knife. I went to take my things out of the back, but Justin's mom stopped me.

"You don't need to take your things out. You're not staying."

I approached Justin with caution. "Hi, are you okay?"

"I'm fine," he answered.

"Can I give you a hug?" I asked, and he agreed.

"Come with me," he said.

I followed him without question as he led me to the guest bathroom. He closed the door behind us and started kissing me passionately. It confused me since he'd gone into a rage a few days earlier.

"I missed you," he whispered, before spinning me around and lifting my blue jean skirt.

I didn't want to have sex with him but went along with it to avoid a scene. I tried pressing him on his sudden change of feelings, but in the end, I just let the whole thing go to focus on our next step.

That same day, Justin's mom dropped us off at Justin's sister's house. Reba lived close by and offered us a place to stay. I felt free for the first time, even though something didn't feel quite "right." I hoped Justin and I would have a clean slate. It was a brand-new start that allowed me to take control of my life. I wanted to look as optimistic as I felt, so I changed into a yellow sundress with sunflowers to wear on my first day. I tried to look my best when I met Reba. I trembled with nervousness but wanted her to know I felt grateful for the place to stay.

We pulled up to a house that looked abandoned. We walked around back where Reba and her family lived. They stayed out of the front rooms to keep out of view of passersby, which made me think they were squatting. The front of the house looked rundown, unlivable even. There were exposed wood beams and a partially collapsed floor. It didn't seem like a safe place to raise a family, but who was I to judge? Reba and her boyfriend, Tony, were friendly when we first met. Reba introduced me to her two small kids. Amanda turned one year old soon after we moved in, and Timmy turned four. Tony tended to the children most of the time. I remember always seeing him holding Amanda and playing games with Timmy. The kids were lucky to have him because Reba emanated a distant and cold vibe. She struggled with her own demons and made sure everyone knew about it.

Reba was a recovering crack/heroin/meth addict and suffered from a mental illness. Justin told me his past was sordid but didn't tell me about his crack/cocaine and alcohol addiction. He drank every day and smoked marijuana, which was acceptable to me, but his new drug addiction to crack cocaine became a whole new animal for me to face. Reba and I remained friendly until I discovered she turned Justin onto meth only a few weeks into our stay. I found the broken lightbulbs they used as pipes, and that evening, my brand-new nightmare began. I confronted them both.

"What are you doing? This is not okay."

Reba spoke up. "You're no princess. It's none of your business what we do together."

I waited for Justin to defend me, but he didn't. Instead, he turned on me and began pushing me backward toward the back door. "I can do whatever the fuck I want. Do you understand?" Justin growled.

I shook my head agreeably, hoping he'd stop pushing me. "Let's just go to bed, okay?" I hoped my amiable demeanor would change his attitude. "I don't want to fight anymore, baby. Okay?"

"You do what you want," he said.

"I'll be waiting for you to join me," I said before he left the room.

I showered and waited for Justin to come in. I fell asleep while waiting but had a rude awakening. He came into the room sometime during the night high on drugs.

"Justin, are you high? I can't believe you'd do that after everything we went through earlier."

Justin exploded. "I told you I do whatever I want!"

He grabbed my arm and dragged my naked body out of bed. He shoved me again, but this time while spurning me out of the house and into the backyard. I banged on the door, "Justin, let me in! I'm naked!"

"Not until you learn not to question me," he responded through the door. "Just get the fuck out of here," he yelled. "Don't make me hurt you."

Naked, humiliated, and bewildered, it stunned me that he could do this to me after everything I went through to get to Florida to be with him. He threatened suicide to get me there, and now that I was there, he treated me like dirt. As I walked away, he opened the door, but instead of inviting me back in, he came out with all my belongings, tossed them into an old swimming pool full of dark green, moldy water, and went back inside. He locked me out for hours before he eventually allowed me to come back in.

The next morning, I went to a secondhand store to replace my clothing. I saw a help wanted sign in the window. I filled out the application and management hired me on the spot, perpetuating my "everything happens for a reason" illusion. I somehow felt grateful that Justin threw my clothes out because I wouldn't have found employment without going to that secondhand store. It was my way of minimizing the abuse, and again, finding a positive in the negative.

We decided to move out of Reba's, so Justin and I went to plan B. Justin's younger sister, Julie, lived nearby. Justin called her, and she agreed to let us stay with her. It relieved me to learn that, unlike Justin and Reba, Julie despised drugs and would never tempt Justin with them. She helped Justin get straight years before we met, but any hope for a sober boyfriend faded when we moved in with Julie. Despite her disdain for the drug community, she inadvertently moved right into its epicenter. Crack cocaine, Justin's enormous demon from his past, beset the area. Addicts now surrounded me, but worst of all, they surrounded Justin, and he couldn't muster up the strength to resist the temptation. Julie and I did what we could to help him, but we couldn't reach him. The whole experience drained me, and mental exhaustion from fighting a losing battle consumed me. Things were more peaceful when I kept my thoughts to myself.

Justin found a job in landscaping while I worked at the thrift store. Julie danced at a local club and didn't take crap from anyone, including Justin. She said things to him that I didn't have the guts to say, and I appreciated the backup. When Justin's paychecks started disappearing, I felt powerless. The burden to pay bills fell to Julie and me. I'd get so angry at Justin for blowing our money, but he didn't care. His "fix" was more important than anything. It was like being married to my father. He blew his money on drugs and alcohol and raged in violence when he didn't have it.

Justin buddied up with a crack addict that lived directly across the street from us. He always offered to get Justin high, and I hated him for it. The neighbor shared custody of his two young daughters who came to visit every other weekend. They were nine and five years old, and I looked forward to their visits, because Justin stayed at home, away from them. Other times, however, he would disappear and literally hide from me. He'd hide in the neighbor's closets or under beds to avoid me when he was bingeing. One night I snapped.

It was a Friday night. I planned to surprise Justin with a romantic evening. I lit candles throughout the house and put-on sexy lingerie, expecting him to be home by six o'clock. I waited for him in the bedroom until ten before I knew he was pulling another disappearing act. After I dressed, I began walking trailer to trailer, looking for him.

The neighbor across the street must have gotten tired of covering for him because he shouted for me to come in without hesitation when I knocked on the door. When I entered, I saw Justin with a crack pipe in his mouth. It was the first time I ever saw Justin using. I sat down next to him and waited for him to finish. Anger filled me, but I didn't make a scene. He handed the pipe to the neighbor to refill. The neighbor put a crumble of rock on top and gave the crack pipe to me, but then Justin intervened.

"Don't give that to her; she doesn't do it," he said.

"Let her try it. She'll probably like it and stop bitching at you for it," suggested the neighbor.

"No, thank you, I'll just hang out."

I was sick of being alone and hurting. I felt defeated and didn't want to fight or resist anymore. I thought if I joined Justin on his binges, he'd be nicer to me. He had been physically violent with me before, but things got worse. After having my head smashed against the floor a few times, I learned that he wouldn't hesitate to knock me around if he thought I'd stand in the way of his fix. I eventually lost my job at the thrift store when I missed a shift after a fight that left me with a black eye.

I desperately wanted to keep Justin away from drugs, and my plan to include myself on his benders backfired horribly. Instead of being more transparent about his drug use, he became more secretive and found a new drug dealer that I didn't know. The neighbor introduced Justin to Vicki, who lived in the same trailer park, only a few streets over. She was the leading supplier for the trailer park. The first time I met her, I asked her not to get high with Justin, and she promised she wouldn't. I should've known that was a lie.

Justin disappeared a few days later, and I bolted to Vicki's trailer. She wasn't home, but Justin and his friend were waiting for her to get back from a drug run. I hid in the bushes and waited about half an hour for her to come back. When I saw her round the corner, I exploded with anger, charged her at full speed, and shoved her as hard as I could. She flew back a few feet onto the ground. The drugs she was carrying flew into the air and landed in a pile of gravel. Vicki searched through the rocks on her hands and knees, to no avail. I thought I'd won the battle, but I underestimated Justin's addiction. He became visibly enraged. I knew he'd make me pay, but I didn't care anymore. He attacked me by pushing me hard to the ground and dousing me with pepper spray before running away. He was going back to the drug house, whether I liked it or not. Justin hoped I wouldn't catch up, but I did, just in time to watch him enter a home. I may have stopped his binge with Vicki, but I knew he'd just go on another. Nothing stood in the way of him getting his fix. I pedaled my bicycle toward the drug house, in fear for my life. I don't know what came over me, but I banged on the door while calling out Justin's name.

"Justin! Come out!"

The person on the other side of one door told me, "You'll be a dead white girl if you don't leave," but it didn't sway me.

I was on a mission and finally heard someone say, "Get the fuck out of here," and saw a large man push Justin out the front door.

"What the fuck are you doing? Are you trying to get us killed?" Justin yelled.

"I'm trying to save your life!" I screamed back at him.

"Look, I'll go home if you just let me get high in peace."

At that moment, I realized I risked my life for nothing. He didn't want me to save him. He got what he wanted and spent the rest of the night doing drugs. After that, I wanted to leave, but I felt helpless. I no longer had a job but didn't want to feel like a failure and go back to Alabama. My feelings for Justin were a deterrent. I still held the illusion that my love for him was so powerful that it could change him. I thought if he experienced real love for the first time, he'd choose love over drugs. But that's not what happened. He continued to smoke his paychecks away and the strain on our finances caused more fights between us. Julie kept to herself but offered up the idea that I join her at the club. Justin thought it was a great idea even though I hated it. I felt out of options, so I considered it. I never wanted to be an exotic dancer, but my limited options left me with no choice. However, Justin had to secure a fake ID for me because I was still a few months shy of my eighteenth birthday.

After a weekend of dancing, it felt like I'd hit my ultimate low. It suddenly occurred to me that I reduced myself to a place I never imagined I'd be, and I refused to ever do it again.

CHAPTER EIGHT:
CODEPENDENT

After another month of watching Justin binge on crack cocaine, I concluded I couldn't do it anymore. I needed to go back to the last place I ever thought I'd return, Alabama. The only way to communicate with anyone in the family was through Granny and Pawpaw, so Justin lashed out in anger and called my grandparents to humiliate me. He told them about the strip club and my experimentation with drugs. I felt beyond furious. How could he betray me that way? I loved him through everything and protected him at all costs.

A physical fight ensued that left me with two black eyes this time. It upset me that Justin called because my Pawpaw didn't approve of the relationship to begin with and wanted Justin to leave me. Pawpaw even offered Justin bribe money to walk away from our relationship, but he didn't. Justin's real motive was to humiliate me. He knew no one knew about our lifestyle and exposed it to everyone.

The next morning, a couple of police officers showed up at my door to conduct a "safety check" at the request of my grandparents. Caught off guard, I stood in front of those men with two black eyes and said all was well. They accepted my answer and told me to enjoy the rest of my day. As soon as I closed the door, I wondered if I made the right decision. Justin showed remorse for the first time. He agreed to go back to Alabama with me and promised to get clean if I'd stay by his side. I believed him when he said he loved me, and I didn't want to mess things up. I thought going back to Alabama was the best decision at the time. I hoped it could be a fresh start, another clean slate. I wanted to finish high school and eventually attend college, while Justin planned to find a steady job in construction. I visualized a great life together away from the drug-infested neighbors.

I moved back to Alabama within a month, but I felt broken, crippled, and defenseless. I felt trapped in a relationship because I promised unconditional love, and I meant it. I felt bound by my own words, not wanting to disappoint Justin the way people had disappointed me. No one fought for me, but I fought for him—if I left him, he'd spiral out of control. I felt if I ended the relationship, I'd be giving up, and I'm no quitter.

I kept Mama in the dark about the horror I went through while away. I didn't tell her about the drugs, even though she introduced me to cigarettes and marijuana before anyone else. Mama once said she'd let me try any illicit drug I wanted if I did it with her, so she could keep me safe. Looking back, I chose not to mention the crack-cocaine use because I feared Mama might be open to doing it with Justin if he ever asked.

Mama had moved into a small brick house in the Alabama countryside while we were away. Finally, a real home. I liked the solitude of the country, even though we had a full house. Justin and I lived with Mama, Michael (20), Christian (13), and York (8). Justin and I liked to explore the woods behind the house to be alone. You can imagine how full a two-bedroom home is with four adults and two rambunctious kids. Things went well for a while until Reba,

Justin's sister, rolled into town. She left Florida for a new life as well and wanted to be near Justin.

I'd been studying for my diploma for a few weeks while Justin worked as a day laborer on construction sites. Soon, he started the silent treatment and disappearing act again. I feared it was a relapse, and sadly, I was right. It turns out that crack is available everywhere and easy to find. Justin and Reba relapsed together. I was seething with the feeling of betrayal by Justin all over again, and I blamed Reba for it all. All was well until she moved into town. Once again, a confrontation ensued between Reba and me, but this time, it turned physical. We scuffled on her front porch, punching, scratching, and pulling each other's hair until Justin intervened. We were both left with bruises, mine worse than hers. She managed to gouge the inside of my lower lip with her fingernails, which left my entire chin black and blue. I felt sick and tired of it all. Justin sided with Reba and moved in with her. I knew he chose drugs over me, and that angered me more. I had it with all the mistreatment and lies. I just wanted an everyday, happy life and a healthy relationship.

Mama told me some truck driver friends were going on the road soon and suggested I go on the trip with them. She said it would give me time to think and help them out with unloading in the process. I'd never met her "truck-driving friends" and felt timid about the idea until I learned they were a married couple. That somehow comforted me, and I thought, what could go wrong? Yet again, things aren't always as they seem.

The couple appeared to be in their mid-to-late thirties. The woman had long brown hair and an athletic build, while the man was a little rougher around the edges with a scruffy beard and potbelly.

The two of them snorted cocaine off a book and smoked crack the entire trip. I wanted to go home by the second day, but again, I felt trapped in an unwanted situation, and I'd be there for five more days. There were no smartphones or Uber yet, and it became more distressing when things got "weird."

The truck could sleep two people, so you can imagine quarters were a little tight with three. The first night I slept alone while the other two took turns driving; the second night, the wife asked if she could bunk with me. I didn't dare put up a fight. I didn't know these people from Adam's house cat and didn't want to do anything to upset them. I was amiable out of fear they'd leave me stranded. I knew all too well it could happen.

By the end of the week, the requests became lascivious. Still shy of my eighteenth birthday, the husband asked me to perform sex acts with his wife. The familiar feeling of powerlessness washed over me, and I begrudgingly did what he asked. Fortunately, he never touched me, but being in such close quarters made it impossible not to see him while he shared intimacy with his wife. I just wanted to go home.

What the fuck was Mama thinking? I wondered. She sent me on a trip with perfect strangers. *What is her deal?* From hitchhikers to lonely older men and everything in between. *Why would she put me in these types of situations?* And then it all became clear to me in the snap of a finger. It's no coincidence that these people were addicts. We'd always been around addicts. I never considered my Mama to be one of them. I knew she tried cocaine and meth, but she went out of her way to make sure I never saw her use except for her daily marijuana habit. From time to time, she would pop speed pills called Yellow Jackets—a counterproductive mixture, to say the least—but I didn't consider either to be "drugs."

I now recognize she always had a penchant for trying new ways to get high, so her doing drugs with her friends didn't fall outside the realm of possibility. On the drive home, I lay in the sleeping cabin and wondered why Mama gave me so much freedom as a child. Now it made sense. Did she want me out of the way so she could do drugs? Did she smoke crack too? It made me question everything. Who did Justin know that could hook him up with drugs? Could it be that my mom had been his source all along? It was all I thought about for days. I kept myself busy trying to put the pieces of the puzzle together. What kind of woman exposes her daughter to so much danger? I just wanted to earn my diploma and move on with life, but something always stood in the way. Had Mama been the obstruction this whole time?

The furious accusations vanished by the end of the trip. I had a new problem on my mind. Reba pressed charges against me for "assaulting" her. She struck a minor, and she filed charges against me? Shouldn't it be the other way around since I was the minor? When the court date rolled around, we all showed up to face the judge. I felt ready to plead my case. I brought pictures of the injuries to my face and planned to let the image speak for itself. My whole body trembled with anxiety. I developed a bizarre coping mechanism over time, which causes me to laugh or smile at inappropriate times. I didn't understand why this happened at the time, but I've since learned that it could be related to an obsessive compulsion disorder (OCD) that I've had since I was four, although it'd take twenty-two years after the hearing before doctors diagnosed me.

When the judge called us forward, Reba and I walked up together. Reba said something under her breath, and I laughed aloud. The judge misinterpreted the laugh to mean that I didn't take the matter seriously and dismissed the case. My shot at justice was right in front of me, and just like that, it went away. I didn't get the chance to defend myself or explain the reason for the laugh. I fucked things up again. If I controlled my laughter, it wouldn't have happened. Again, I blamed myself for everything.

I fell deeper into the rabbit hole of codependency and doubled down on my pursuit to make things work, believing Justin when he said everything would be okay. He wanted to reconcile now that I admitted my fault. He asked me to forgive Reba, and I agreed. Although we reunited, the relationship never felt the same. I found ways to stay away from Reba and focus my energy on my diploma.

I attended a GED program and prepared myself to take the test within five weeks. My desire to do better than Mama motivated me to complete the course. I kept going out of sheer determination to achieve this goal and move out of state. I knew I'd have a better shot at finding decent employment with a degree. I just needed to find the money to take the test first.

Justin's other sister, Julie, moved to New Hampshire, so he decided to move with her. He argued that he needed a substantial change, but I planted my feet in Alabama until I passed that test. I didn't want to quit after coming so far. After some discussion, Justin and I agreed I'd move up after my GED test. He promised to get himself settled in and have things ready for me in a few months. It made me sad to see him go, but it was a price I was willing to pay. I'd never finished anything in my life, and that needed to change.

I worked as a dishwasher at a small soul food restaurant in town to save up for the test. It took me a month. I felt confident the night of the test since I'd flown through the learning material in class. I waited six long weeks for the test results to come in. My hands trembled as I ripped the envelope and unfolded the results. I read the word "CONGRATULATIONS," and I knew I passed. I achieved my goal and waited for my diploma to come in the mail. It was time to prepare for my long journey from Alabama to New Hampshire.

CHAPTER NINE:
FIGHT OR FLIGHT

The plane touched down in unfamiliar territory. I knew I'd leave Alabama, but I never dreamed I'd get that far away. Two thousand seven hundred and forty-three miles, to be exact. I exited the terminal with luggage in tow. The brisk air caught me off guard. My face never felt wind so cold. Chills trickled down my back as my body tried to adjust to the temperature. I felt thankful to have a coat and gloves but quickly noticed the much thicker gloves, hats, and scarves the locals were wearing. My ears froze, and my thin, shoulder-length blonde hair did nothing to protect them.

I sat on the first bench I came across and fumbled through my bag for my cigarettes, anxious to light up. I hated flying, even more so in the middle of turbulent weather. I took a long drag from the cigarette, closed my eyes, and released a smoke-filled breath. I felt lucky to be alive. I opened my eyes and smiled; I wasn't in small-town Alabama anymore. I saw the rushing traffic and noticed northeastern accents. I was in a whole new world, and it was my new home. My heart was pounding as I watched the cars drive by. I felt apprehensive and exhilarated at the same time. This move was a new chapter in my life—another opportunity for change. After everything I'd been through, I'd been preparing for this moment my entire life.

As a young girl, I daydreamed about having a job, my own money, my own apartment, and my very own life. It was a pivotal time for me because I finally had control over my finances, and I officially gained independence.

Julie was kind enough to pick me up from the airport. The ride to her apartment was surreal. I stared at the passing license plates, still in disbelief that I moved to New Hampshire. Justin had been there only a couple of months and said Julie was helping him stay clean. He arranged for us to stay with her rent-free until we could both find jobs and save up for a place of our own.

The car slowed and then stopped in front of a blue two-story duplex. I stepped out and the snow crunched beneath my boots as I walked to the rear to get my bag. I looked around and saw a few employment opportunities within walking distance. I turned back to the house to see Justin standing in the doorway. I didn't have the same excitement to see him as I did before. I still cared for him, but the flame had dimmed. I approached him more guarded and was relentless about making a positive change in my life. I was optimistic about my future but knew Justin could relapse at any time. This time, however, I wouldn't be going along for the ride. Another drug relapse was my only deal-breaker. I stepped into the kitchen, where Justin greeted me with a smile and half-hearted, "Hello."

I put my bags down and reached out for a hug that I wasn't sure he would give. He put his arm out, and I knew it was safe for me to move in closer.

"I'm so happy to see you," I whispered in his ear.

"I'm happy to see you too."

I could tell he was in a mood, so I tried not to provoke him by staying out of his way. Besides Justin's drug and alcohol abuse, I was not aware of any mental illness, but his display of erratic behavior over time caused me to wonder.

The first night was the longest. I contended with a million thoughts racing through my brain. *How long will it take to save money? Where will we move? Will things be better between Justin and me?* My future was now up to me to create. The excitement of stepping out into my new world kept me awake. I quietly planned my next steps while lying in bed when Justin's voice broke the silence.

"What are you thinking about?"

"Getting a job. I saw a couple of places nearby." I yawned.

"Make sure it's within walking distance because we don't have a car yet."

"I'm going to pick up as many job applications as I can first thing tomorrow morning, starting with the convenience store across the street."

"That's a good idea. I'll be working late with the landscaping company."

I acknowledged with an "okay" and turned over to fall asleep.

I woke up early, steadfast in my goal of independence. I had worked a few jobs in Alabama, but my life's instability made it impossible to hold a position anywhere too long. Now, I was finally in charge of my destiny, and I planned to take it by the horns. I dreamt about this moment for years. Through all the hardships and pain, I knew this time would come. Being in New Hampshire was my opportunity to change my life, and I wasn't going to blow it. I was eighteen with my whole life in front of me, and I wanted to prepare to do it independently.

I grabbed my coat and boots and headed out the door into the cold, snowy weather. I walked across the street with a mission to return with a job. I walked into the convenience store, and a bell above the door sounded a loud "DING." I smiled at the clerk behind the counter and asked if they were hiring. The clerk said he didn't know, but the manager would be back soon. I asked for an application anyway.

"Sure," the clerk said. "You can fill it out here if you want to wait for the manager. His name is Gil."

I thanked him and propped up against a stack of boxes and started filling out the application. To signify my new beginning, I dropped my childhood nickname, Eve, and wrote my full government name, Yvonne. I planned to lose my southern accent as quickly as possible. I felt like a new person. It felt weird putting "Yvonne" on the application since no one ever called me that. It felt like I was pretending to be someone I wasn't, and it took a while for me to acclimate to it. A few minutes later, Gil returned.

The clerk pointed to me and said, "She's here about a job."

Gil waved and then introduced himself. "Hi, I'm Gil."

"Hi, Gil, I'm Yvonne. I stopped by to ask if you're hiring." I said with a firm handshake.

"Nice grip. We need a second-shift cashier. Are you interested?"

I enthusiastically told him I'd start right away, and he said I could start training that day on second shift. I was so proud of myself as I walked back across the street. I landed a job at my first stop and looked forward to starting. Gil said he'd promote me to assistant manager if I did well, and it was an opportunity to make new friends. I returned at three o'clock to start my new career.

After six months or so, my relationship with Justin was still a challenge. I did my best to keep the peace, but we were on rocky ground. He said he was clean from hard drugs, but he still drank all the time and continued verbally abusing me. He struggled to make it home after work most nights, which caused frequent arguments that took their toll. I was in a new world with no friends or family, and Justin was still an abuser. I hoped the move would change things, but sadly, it didn't. The abuse was "only" emotional and verbal at this point, but I'd learned from our time in Florida that he could get physical, so it was best not to provoke him. We didn't have open communication, so I kept my feelings to myself. I felt lonely, but most of all, I felt frustrated. "Why wouldn't Justin listen to me?

Why wouldn't he let me love him? Why couldn't he love me?" I asked myself.

Within six or seven months of my arrival, Justin and I moved into an apartment together just over the border in Maine and bought a flivver 1989 Honda Civic for three hundred bucks. The car burned oil, leaving a plume of black smoke behind us everywhere we went, but it got us to and from work. Since I worked the second shift, Justin had a lot of time on his hands, and now he had a car. I never trusted him, but when his friend from the old Florida drug neighborhood came to visit, I knew it was the first stage of failure for us. I knew Justin would relapse, and I was right, but my reaction was different this time. My tolerance for it went down to zero.

Now that I worked a full-time job, I knew it was my opportunity to get out. When a coworker gave me a choice to move in with her, I took it. I felt disappointed about Justin's relapse but came to accept that he'd never love me as much as he loved his drugs. I didn't deserve to be in second place. The day I left was one of our worst days. Torn between my feelings and doing the right thing, I just couldn't take his cruelty any longer. After a 24-hour binge, he came home in a terrible mood and was none too pleased to find me packing a bag.

"What the fuck are you doing?"

"I'm moving out, Justin. I can't take this anymore."

"Where do you think you're going?"

"I have a place to go. Don't you worry about it."

"Yeah, you're probably going to shack up with some guy because that's all you know how to do."

"Why do you care? You don't even come home at night! You'd rather be out getting high than at home with me, and I'm done!"

As usual, he didn't care what I said and continued spewing hateful things at me. In the middle of the argument, the house phone rang. I picked up the phone angrily.

"Hello?"

"Eve?"

"Mama?" I barely heard her voice from the crying.

"Mama, is that you?"

"Yes, doll, it's me. I'm sorry, but I have terrible news."

"What's wrong, Mama? Is it Granny or Pawpaw?" I asked in fear.

"No, honey, it's your Uncle Marty."

"What happened?"

"He was shot and killed last night."

"What? Uncle Marty?" I started to cry and looked up at Justin.

I was devastated and shocked. Justin and I spent the weekend with him in Alabama a few months earlier, and I wished it had been a better visit. We argued the entire trip. With the phone still to my ear, I turned to Justin and said, "Marty is dead. Marty got murdered."

I thought he'd be remorseful or have some compassion about the situation. He just spent the weekend with my uncle; surely the news would hit him as hard as it hit me. But his response floored me.

He looked me dead in the face as I sobbed and said, "That's what you get for being a bitch."

I was in disbelief. *Did he just say what he said*? I wondered.

"What did you just say to me?" I asked.

"That's what you get for being a cunty bitch. It's your fault he's dead."

"What the actual fuck? Do you have a kind bone in your body? If so, I never experienced it."

We began screaming at one another, and I told Mama I'd call her back. Our voices grew louder and louder. Enraged, I went on to say to him that I was sick of his drug and alcohol addiction. I was sick of his vengeful spirit. This time, he responded with violence, grabbing me by the hair and throwing me to the ground. He sat on top of me and refused to let me up. I was screaming bloody murder when I heard the police knocking at the door.

"This is the police department. Do you need assistance?"

Justin had me pinned to the floor and told me to tell them I was okay.

"I'm okay; I just want to go to bed," I pleaded. "Just go away!" I shouted, hoping Justin would have some mercy on me after they left.

Anyone with a brain would've known I was lying. Through my tears, I said to the officers again, "I just want to go to bed. Please, everything is okay." I begged.

"If you don't open the door, we're going to knock it down!" the police threatened.

Justin stood over me with a thirteen-inch television and threatened to bash my head in. I begged the police, "Please, don't do that. I'm begging you! Just go away!"

The most surprising part is they did. The police walked away while I was bleeding on the other side of the door. While Justin held me against my will, the police just turned around and left me there. Law enforcement has let me down more than once, but this situation had a lasting impact on me. This failure cemented my distorted belief that I wasn't worth protecting, and Justin taunted me with it as he set the TV aside.

"I told you no one would save you," he snarled as he straddled my battered body.

Flabbergasted and in shock, my spirit felt desecrated. I didn't bother cleaning the blood from my face and arms. I just wanted the night to be over. He held me down by my wrists.

"Justin, please let me up. They're gone now."

"I'll let you up when I'm ready," he said nastily.

"I just want to go to bed, please, just let me go to bed."

"Are you going to mouth off again?"

"No, I just want to sleep."

After a final squeeze to my wrists, he let me loose, and I picked myself up off the floor. I went straight to the bedroom to lie down. I didn't wash my face or bother changing clothes. Justin followed close behind and demanded sex from me, so I lay there as he violated me once more. His touch, once craved, now disgusted me, and I just wanted to fall asleep. I didn't want to spend another day in the relationship.

The next morning, I packed a few things and told Justin I was going to the airport under the ruse of attending Marty's funeral. What he didn't know was that I scheduled my flight for the next day. Instead of going to Alabama right away, I brought a few belongings to my coworker's, Leigh's house. Before the murder even happened, Leigh was on the schedule with me one day when Justin came in, yelling obscenities at me. Leigh made Justin leave and offered her spare room to me if I ever needed to get out fast. I appreciated the safe place and now had a reason to take her up on her offer.

In my situation, the outside world remained clueless about the abuse (sexual, physical, mental), and it felt normal. In my family, there's a pervasive belief in victim-blaming, so I had nowhere to turn. Everyone I told about my abuse as a child minimized the behavior or denied that it happened at all, so as a result, I grew up feeling very alone and suffered greatly because no one reciprocated the unconditional loyalty they demanded from me.

The people surrounding me were the very ones feeding me poisonous lies to protect the perpetrators. Leigh's quick response was a breath of fresh air. I finally felt like someone was in my corner. It was the first time I left Justin, so I didn't know how he would react. I feared he'd show up there just to cause trouble. I didn't feel safe at Leigh's place or the store, but I needed my job more than ever now, so I stayed for the financial security.

The flight to Alabama for Marty's funeral was difficult. Not only was I grieving the loss of my uncle, but I was still reeling over everything that happened with Justin. I acknowledged that as terrible as he treated me, I always loved him and felt sad that the relationship was over.

When I got to Alabama, I kept all the traumas with Justin to myself. The pain in Mama's face was clear when I saw her in baggage claim. Her eyes were billowy from days of grieving the loss of her baby brother. I wrapped my arms around her, and tears began falling again. Everyone in the family was in shock. Why Marty?

As authorities released facts of the case, we learned the entire event was even more horrendous than we feared. We learned that Uncle Marty and his family were victims of a home invasion by a stranger. Allegedly, the man's motive was robbery, but my immediate family outwardly wondered if he went there with the intent to kill Uncle Marty for other reasons. Regardless, the details of that night are too terrible to even believe. The rest of the details that happened that night aren't my story to tell, so I'll leave it there.

During the funeral, the entire family was distraught. We all wanted to wrap our arms around Aunt Lori and their two young children, but they were all still in shock and understandably withdrawn. Unfortunately, my family's behavior after this tragedy split our family apart rather than bringing us closer. Early on, some family members openly suspected that Aunt Lori might have known the killer and accused her of having more information, which devastated Aunt Lori. Sadly, victim-blaming is a common occurrence, and my family gave Lori the standard treatment.

They believed my uncle's murder was her fault in some way, and they shunned her from the family. Lori stayed away from everyone in our family from that time on, and I can't blame her. I haven't seen her in person since before the murder, which happened in May 1998. Fortunately, authorities caught the killer right away, a jury convicted him, and as of September 29th, 2020, he was sitting on death row at St. Clair Correctional Facility in Alabama.

Despite all the family drama and conspiracy theories, nothing could keep me distracted from my problems waiting back in Maine. I secretly moved out of my apartment by packing as many clothes as possible into my travel bag and left everything else behind. In doing so, I relinquished possession of my physical property (furniture, TV, mattress and box spring, food, and personal care products like shampoo and conditioner). I made sure he didn't suspect my plan to abandon the apartment we shared for the past three months because he'd inevitably sabotage my attempt.

CHAPTER TEN:
NEGATIVE CONSEQUENCES

After Marty's funeral, I returned to Leigh's house without incident, as planned. Justin knew I was due to arrive back that day, so it wouldn't be long for him to realize I wasn't coming home. Within a week, he found out where I lived and was in the front yard, yelling and screaming.

"Eve, please don't do this to me! I thought you loved me! Please don't leave me!"

Leigh and I watched from her second story bedroom window. "Do you want me to call the police?" Leigh asked.

"No, he might get arrested," I feared aloud.

"So, what! He might be dangerous!" Leigh reminded me.

"I know, I know. If he tries to come into the house, we'll call. Otherwise, I'm just going to ignore him until he goes away."

Justin continued. "Eve, please come home. I promise I've changed."

He only wanted me around when it was convenient for him. I knew he only wanted me back because he controlled me, but I'd had enough. I accepted that he'd return to his old ways if I went back, and I refused to fall for it. I'd become the sounding board for his rage, and it needed to change.

"GO AWAY, Justin!" I yelled out the window.

Leigh ran back into the room. "I thought you're ignoring him?"

"I know, I just want him to leave me alone. I'm sick of him." I turned back to the window. "Justin, I don't want anything to do with you. Leave now, or I'm calling the police!"

He kept begging me to come out and talk to him.

"No, Justin. I'm not talking anymore. It's over. Leave now!"

I don't know how I summoned the strength to resist him. In the past, I'd run out the door to give him a second chance, but this time, I stood my ground. Thankfully, he wasn't up for a fight either and left without further incident after about half an hour.

I took a week off work to mourn my Uncle Marty but looked forward to going back. I needed a good distraction from all the pain I felt. I just hoped Justin would leave me alone. My first night back at work started uneventfully but ended with a bang. About two hours before my shift ended, I saw a familiar car pull up to the gas pumps. It was Justin and his drug friend from Florida. I continued helping customers while waiting for Justin to come inside to pay. I became suspicious that he was up to no good when he didn't come inside after pumping his gas. He appeared to be waiting for the store to clear out.

Finally, the last customer left, and I saw Justin and his friend make their way toward the store. I nervously said hi to them when they walked in and watched as they quietly went to the back of the store. I turned my attention to another customer who walked in and didn't notice Justin and his friend making their way to the with bottles of orange juice and a couple of beer cases. In the middle of the customer transaction, I was blindsided by cold orange juice hitting my face. Justin opened the juice and splashed me before emptying the gallon container onto the counter and cash register.

Justin and his friend continued ransacking the aisles and destroying the store.

After a scary three-or-four-minute ordeal, Justin ran out of the store with a couple of cases of beer, a handful of disposable cameras, and a stolen tank of gas. I didn't call the police, though now I wish I had. At the time, I was simply happy they left. I locked the door, cleaned up the mess and hoped they wouldn't come back before my shift ended. I didn't trust him not to return to Leigh's apartment, so he left me no choice but to find another place to live. This time, I made sure he couldn't find me. I feared what he could do to me, but more than that, I needed to put space between us so he couldn't manipulate me to come back. Yes, I was fed up, but I still loved him and didn't feel strong enough to be around him at all.

At the time, I still felt a sense of protectiveness and responsibility for Justin's well-being, so I never even considered calling authorities that night. I just cleaned up the mess and hoped the juice didn't ruin the cash register. Fortunately, the register still functioned, and I was able to restore the store to its earlier condition. Gil was none the wiser.

The next morning, I decided to go back to our apartment after Justin left for work to collect a few important documents I left behind. As soon as I opened the front door, the stench of urine blasted my senses. I walked through the kitchen, and to the bedroom, where Justin had used scissors to cut up and pour mustard over all my remaining clothing. I ran to the closet, praying he hadn't discovered my birth certificate and social security card. When I made it to the living room, I found our Rent-A-Center couch, drenched in Justin's urine, and a cable Pay-Per-View porno video on the television. Justin wanted to sabotage me. He ordered the movies, just to leave me with the bill. He was a psychopath to me, and I started to wonder why I ever loved him at all. Especially after his second attempt to get me fired from my job about two months later.

Justin showed up at the store, begging me to ride with him while I was on a quick break. I agreed to sit in the car and talk if we didn't leave the parking lot. I just wanted to end the madness. I thought if I did what he wanted; it would keep him calm. He said he wouldn't leave the parking lot, and I fell for it. It was the dead of winter. It was freezing, with snow-covered ground. I went without my winter coat, not expecting to stay long. As soon as I closed the door, Justin quickly reversed the car and sped out of the parking lot, ignoring my pleas to stop.

"Justin, STOP! What are you doing? You promised you wouldn't leave the parking lot," I yelled.

"You promised you'd never leave me. How does it feel to be lied to?"

He drove further away from the store while spewing obscenities at me.

"It's your fucking fault all of this is happening! All you had to do was mind your own fucking business, and everything would have been okay," he screamed at me.

"Justin, what the fuck are you talking about?" I felt confused about where he was going with the conversation. "I left because of the things you said when Marty died. I can never forgive you for that."

Justin slammed on the brakes and stopped in the middle of the street. He peered at me angrily. "So, you're saying you're not going to give me another chance?"

I sat silent for a moment out of fear of Justin's unpredictability. By this time, he had driven at least two miles away from the store, and I needed to convince him to take me back.

"Justin, we can talk about it after I get out of work, but right now, you have to take me back to the store, so I don't get fired."

"Is that all you fucking care about, Eve? Your worthless fucking job? You must love your job more than you love me since that's all you want to fucking discuss with me! I'm not taking you back; you can fucking walk back for all I care."

"Please just take me back, and we'll talk later, okay?"

"Get the fuck out of the car, Eve."

"Justin, I don't have a coat. I'll freeze out there!"

Justin grabbed me by my uniform shirt and pulled me nose to nose with him, while screaming, "I don't care. GET THE FUCK OUT OF THE CAR!" He reached over me and pulled the passenger door handle to open the door. "If you're not going to get out on your own, I'll fucking push you out!"

I tried to hold onto the car seat, but he overpowered me and managed to push me out of the car and onto the icy road before speeding away. I stood speechless for a moment, half expecting him to turn around to come back for me, but I watched his taillights eventually fade out of sight. It was a 45-minute grueling walk to make it back to the store, just as my shift was ending. Luckily for me, I still had a job when I returned, but now that Justin reappeared at the store, it left me no choice but to find a new job.

For the time being, I stayed focused on saving money and becoming more independent. My first goal was to save up for my first car. After a few months, I gave it a go when I saw the cutest 1994 periwinkle blue VW Jetta sitting on a lot. All it took was a $500 deposit, and she was mine. Having reliable transportation meant I could expand my job search, so I contacted a staffing agency. I was nineteen years old and up for anything.

After several interviews and a typing test, the agency offered me various full-time temporary positions that could become permanent, with decent pay. The most exciting opportunity was a temporary position as a typesetter at our local newspaper, *The Daily Democrat*. My job was to retype potential stories and articles into a computer software program for editors to review before sending them to print.

By the end of 1998, I had honed my typing skills to 90 words per minute, which opened more employment opportunities. I went on to work on a lightbulb manufacturer assembly line and sorted mail in the mailroom of a large insurance company, but the best was the opportunity to work for an airline. The airline bought a half dozen or so Boeing 727s that needed heavy maintenance for airworthiness certification. I worked in a giant hangar as a data processor, inputting plane parts and serial numbers into an inventory database. When I completed that project, I transitioned to the records department, where I tracked the hours and cycles for each plane per the FAA guidelines.

My job was to ensure that nothing was "overflown," which means I ensured the jet-techs completed maintenance items within a specific time period. The airline could get a fine depending on the out-of-date task. It was a big responsibility, and I loved it. Mechanics disassembled the planes one by one and overhauled the jet engines, fixed landing gear, and repaired fuselages. I helped in the maintenance department as needed, distributing parts to the plane technicians. It was a fascinating place to be.

***

After moving to New Hampshire, I lost contact with most of my family except for the occasional call from Mama. My brothers were twenty-one, thirteen, and eight when I moved, so I lost communication with them too. Mama moved around so much it was hard to keep track. Even if I knew where she was, Mama couldn't afford a phone, so I wouldn't be able to reach her anyway. I only got to talk to them if I called Granny and Pawpaw's house and they happened to be there. Otherwise, I didn't know where they lived, how they were doing, or what was going on around them. It may sound cruel, but I don't mean it in the dismissive way that it may imply, but I followed the "out of sight, out of mind" mantra for my sanity. Selfishly, I was afraid to know what was going on because I didn't want to worry about things that were out of my control. I was so out of touch that I missed the births of all my nieces and nephews. I didn't know Christian was married for ten years or that my brothers moved back with my dad for a while after my move to New Hampshire. Flared tempers forced my brothers to separate from Daddy again.

During a rare call, Mama bragged that she allowed my nine-year-old brother, York, to get a tattoo on his hand.

"Did you know York got a tattoo?"

"What?" I exclaimed. *Do I hear this?* "Why would you allow that?"

"He wanted a tattoo like his big brother," she casually responded.

"Where did he get it?" I asked out of curiosity. Not that it mattered.

"He got a cross on his hand like his big brother."

As a mom myself, I cannot fathom allowing a nine-year-old to get a tattoo. Sadly, all my brothers got homemade tattoos with equipment made from needles, pen ink, and batteries well before the legal age of eighteen, and that was okay with my mom. I tuned out what was happening back at home because it was just another situation out of my control.

I was grateful to be away from all the drama, but it was only temporary; other problems were ahead of me. I planned to fly home for Thanksgiving in 1998 and dreaded sitting across the table from my pervert uncle, Lou. He acted like nothing ever happened, and everyone in the family went right along with it. It troubled me to learn he was dating a woman named Bev with three girls aged ten through thirteen. I'd be meeting her for the first time at Thanksgiving dinner, and I felt compelled to tell her all about what Lou did to me.

During the flight to Georgia, I deliberated my decision. *Was telling Bev the right thing? What if it caused trouble? What if she didn't believe me? Even worse, what if she did believe me and did nothing about it?* By the time my plane touched down, I'd made up my mind. I was going through with it. If something did happen to any of her daughters, I'd be complicit. Mama picked me up from the airport, and I greeted her with a long bear hug.

"It's so good to see you, Mama. How are you?"

"I'm okay, doll, I've just been missing you is all."

119

"I've missed you too, Mama."

I smiled at her as she unlocked the back of Pawpaw's classic burgundy Oldsmobile Cutlass Supreme, and I tossed my bag in the trunk. It was a beautiful sunny day. Grandma's house was forty-five minutes away, so it was a good time to talk to Mama about my intention to confront Lou's new girlfriend, Bev.

I stared out the window at the trees whizzing by, appreciating the beauty of the magnificent centuries-old Oak trees. Mama rolled down her window to flick her cigarette ashes out.

"Mom, do you remember what I told you about Lou?"

Mama looked over at me, her long brunette hair twisting in the wind; and with a deep sigh, acknowledged, "Yes, I do. I still hate him for doing that to you."

"Well, I need to tell Bev what happened because of her daughters. Do you think I should do it?"

Mama sat quietly for a moment, and I gave her the space to ponder the question. She took a long drag of her cigarette and flicked more ashes into the wind. She exhaled a cloud of smoke that resembled a thought bubble, and I wished I could read her mind.

"Well, I'd support it, because Lou has lost his ever-loving mind."

Her comment surprised me. "Why do you say that?"

"He's just been doing some bizarre shit."

My attention tore away from the passing cars and focused on Mama, "Like what?"

"Like trying to have sex with Melody and me."

"What? When did this start?" I asked fervently.

"A couple of months ago." She said casually. But it was her next statement that floored me. "I think it runs in the family."

Her words hit me like a ton of bricks. It was the first time I ever heard Mama acknowledge our disturbing family history.

"Who else do you think is messed up?" I genuinely wanted to know.

Before this conversation, Mama only talked about how great her childhood was, so I listened intently, waiting for her to reveal the truth.

"Your Pawpaw hasn't been acting right either."

"How do you mean?"

"Just make sure you lock the bathroom door when you shower. Pawpaw has been peeking in on the women when they shower."

I reacted with an emphatic, "What?"

I don't know why the news shocked me. I'd known this about Pawpaw since he touched me at the age of eleven. *What is wrong with the men in my family?*

The 45-minute drive flew by, and before I knew it, we pulled into Granny and Pawpaw's driveway. My heart pounded when I saw that Bev and Lou were already there. As I stepped onto the porch, I saw Lou through the small window on the door. I contemplated how to greet him and opted for brief. I opened the door, and Lou greeted me.

"Hey, girl! Welcome home!"

"Thanks. Good to see you."

"Good to see you too, baby girl."

I hurried past him and into the kitchen, where Bev was standing talking to my grandma.

"Hey, Granny, I'm here!"

"Hey, sweetie, I'm so glad to see you."

I dropped my bags to give her a big hug and kiss. "The food smells delicious! I can't wait for your biscuits!"

Granny opened the oven to show me the fresh batch she already had going for me. Bev approached me to introduce herself. She was a heavy woman with short, curly brunette hair.

"Well, hey, Eve. It's so nice to meet you finally."

I wondered if she'd still feel that way after our little chat later, but for the moment, I was polite. "It's good to meet you too. Where's Pawpaw?"

"He's sitting by the fireplace, watching a Western."

I walked into the den to find Pawpaw just where Granny said he would be, in his recliner by the wood burning fireplace. I love the smell of the wood and glow of the embers.

"Hey, Pawpaw. Look who finally arrived."

I smiled at him as I bent down to hug him and kiss him on his cheek. He greeted me with the usual, "Hey, buttercup, pudding pie, with a cherry on top."

He rose from his brown recliner to hug me and tried to graze my breast, but I blocked him with my arm. *Some things never change*, I thought. But then again, some things do. Granny and Pawpaw's house felt different this time. Like I lifted the wool from my eyes and was seeing people for who they truly were. I realized that this house wasn't a haven; it was a mental health nightmare disguised as a perfectly normal, tight-knit family. Lou shuffled around the house, trying to make conversation with me. I engaged in as little small talk as possible before transitioning back to the kitchen with all the women.

I turned the corner to the hallway and was relieved to see my mom's sister, Aunt Melody, and her family arrive. Melody and I have always been close and enjoyed the time we spent together. Melody is the baby girl and the comedian of the sisters. She has beautiful green/hazel eyes and goes out of her way to look her best, especially on Thanksgiving.

"Hey! I'm so glad you finally made it!" I said as Melody threw her arms around me.

"Me too! How was your flight?" she responded as she squeezed me tight.

"Oh, it was uneventful. Just the way a flight should be." I grabbed her by the hand. "Come with me. I need to put my bags in my room."

Melody and I walked down the hallway to the first room on the left. It was the same room I slept in every time I visited my

122

grandparents. It still felt like "my" room. Melody followed me in and shut the door behind us.

"Is it true about Lou and Grandpa?"

"Your mom must have told you, huh?"

"Yes, she did. Did it happen to you too?"

She just looked at me and confirmed with a simple nod of the head.

"Oh, my God. That's insane."

"I know, right?"

"I'm telling Bev about Lou. She needs to know the truth," I blurted out.

"I think you should. Tell Bev not to trust Lou or Pawpaw around her girls," Melody counseled.

I appreciated the support but wondered at the same time why no one else had told Bev. I felt frustrated that my family didn't understand the degree of danger those girls were in, but I didn't have time to think about that either. I was mulling over what to say to Bev. I'd only talked to Granny about what happened a few months earlier, and her response hurt me.

"Well, he's a different person now, so it doesn't matter."

Those words, "it doesn't matter," echo through my mind to this day. I was nineteen years old and still hoping my family would comfort me, to no avail. Granny gave me the message that what Lou did to me didn't matter because he "changed." In Granny's mind, I should just forgive and forget. That's what I tried to do as a fourteen-year-old girl, but as a nineteen-year-old woman, I realized I hadn't forgiven him at all.

Granny announced it was dinnertime, and I came back from my reverie trip down memory lane. Thanksgiving dinner didn't taste the same. Even Grandma's treasured buttermilk biscuits. It was as though the family's blasé attitude toward child sexual abuse and incest tainted everything, even Granny's cooking. After dinner, Pawpaw, Lou, and a few other family members went to the garage to play music. Pawpaw started the jam session with some piano playing, and then others joined in with their guitars.

I come from a musical family, which is the only trait I got from them. It was always my favorite part of the trip. I loved to sing but didn't have the confidence to sing in front of anyone else, including family. Usually, I'd make my way to the garage to listen to the jam session, but again, this time felt different. I didn't want to be around my Pawpaw or Lou. The mere sight of them made me angry. I felt something boiling inside that wouldn't stay pent up.

A sense of purpose and a biting urgency to protect the daughters of a woman I didn't know overtook me. I did everything in my power to protect them, so instead of following the parade of people to the garage, I found Bev on the front porch smoking a cigarette.

CHAPTER ELEVEN:
THE MOMENT OF TRUTH

It was the moment I had been waiting for. I sat next to Bev on the porch swing. We swayed back and forth for a few minutes, making small talk before I built up the courage to say what I needed to tell her.

"Your girls seem sweet," I said.

"They're a handful, let me tell you."

I chuckled a little. "I'm sure they are."

After another brief silence, I continued. "So, there's something I need to tell you about Lou. Before I say it, I need you to understand the only reason I'm telling you is so you can protect your children."

"I understand," she said casually.

"What you choose to do with the information after you have it is up to you, but I have to tell you that Lou sexually abused me when I was thirteen, so please keep a close eye on your girls."

Her lack of reaction didn't surprise me, but I waited, hoping for a response.

"Did you hear what I just told you?"

"Yes. I'm thinking about my response."

"Okay, well, take your time." What Bev said next stunned me.

"My girls already told me he tried something with them."

"Oh, my God. You know he's already tried?"

"Yeah, so I put locks on the inside of their bedroom doors to keep him out."

I'm sure I looked stunned because she looked at me a bit perplexed.

"Are you fucking kidding me?" I asked her. "It's your responsibility to protect those girls and putting a lock on the inside of the door isn't enough. If you don't protect your daughters, they will resent you for it in the end."

"Well, he didn't get to them, so the locks will be fine. I love Lou and don't know what I'd do without him."

I felt sick to my stomach. I was seeing a mother choose a pedophile over the safety of her children. Her response disgusted me so much that I wanted nothing more to do with her. I said my piece, and that's all I had the power to do.

"Well, I told you. If anything happens, it's going to be on you."

I stood up and walked back inside. I sat by the fireplace and contemplated what the backlash would be for telling Bev my secret. Not that I cared since I was flying out the next morning. I came to speak my truth, and sometimes the truth hurts.

The following day, as I packed my bags to head back to the bitter cold of New Hampshire, my mind was still reeling from my conversation with Bev. When I left the house, I felt solace in knowing I was flying away from that place. Bev's nonchalant attitude about Uncle Lou's pedophilia reminded me of how Mama did not protect me, and it infuriated me. I had the opportunity to talk to Mama about it on the ride back to the airport, but I didn't see the point. I took a considerable risk to tell Bev, and it felt like another door slammed in my face. I didn't have the energy to get into it with Mama, so I stuffed the anger deep down, enlarging the crater of pain created in my childhood. My time in Georgia reminded me of how much I'd grown since being away. It renewed my determination to make a better life for myself. I didn't intend to think about it anymore. It was time to refocus my energy on my next mission, erasing Justin from my life completely. I started by moving out of Leigh's apartment.

I moved to another small town in New Hampshire, close to the Maine border, and took the first option I found, a rundown boarding house named the HB Boarding House. It was the last place Justin would expect me to go because it was known for housing drug addicts, prostitutes, and felons. There was a bar with a couple of pool tables on the first floor where most of the residents spent time together. My skin crawled every time I walked into the building. All I did was keep my head down and walk up the three flights of stairs to my room.

The tiny, cold room had dark blue painted wood floors, white walls, and a small window with a view of a strip mall and a little Italian restaurant. It didn't have a television, just a twin-size bed, a dresser for my clothing, and a wooden chair sitting in the corner. The shared bathroom and shower were in the hall for all residents on my floor to use. I was not too fond of it and only showered when I had no other choice. I tried not to think about the sheets and blankets I slept on at night.

I reminded myself that the situation was only temporary, and I'd find a way out. I kept my distance from everyone, because they did drugs openly at the bar and in the hallway. More than once, I stepped over people high on heroin in the stairwell. I considered reaching out to Justin to reconcile. I left him because of his addiction just to move into a house full of drug addict strangers. I started feeling like a hypocrite, but then I reminded myself that I left Justin over more than just his drug addiction. He was mentally, emotionally, physically, and sexually abusive toward me. I told myself that these people were drifters—not my monkeys, not my circus.

In the meantime, the airline hired me full time as the maintenance planner, and I loved it. Instead of merely tracking when the landing gear, engines, and other parts needed maintenance, my job was to write out the work orders for the technicians to remove and replace landing gear, engines, avionics, and other time-limited components—a once-in-a-lifetime opportunity, to be sure. The promotion came with a significant raise, so within three months, I moved out of the boarding house and into my first apartment alone, giving me complete independence.

It was a small one-bedroom apartment on the second floor with a cute sun porch on Mt. Vernon Street. It'd been months since Justin tried to contact me, but I still watched my back out of fear he'd come back. I didn't live in total peace, but my mood was lighter. I made a couple of friends and started dating a jet-tech named Brent. He and I met during my time in the parts room. We both worked twelve to fourteen hours a day. We joked that our first date was at McDonald's because that's the first place we ate lunch alone together. Work lunches progressed to spending time outside of work, and we grew closer.

Brent was the change I needed. He was handsome, funny, caring, loyal, and the first man to treat me with respect and show me what having a real family is like. Brent praised his mother and spoke about his father with love and care. He was close to his family, and I looked forward to experiencing those loving relationships. His parents had divorced but remained close friends.

Anne, his mom, remarried a couple of years later, but John, his dad, chose to stay single. John had a stroke several years earlier and never regained full use of his left side, so Anne stayed around to help. It impressed me that John had dinner with Anne and her husband all the time, and the three of them were great friends. It was quite different from my experience. My dad couldn't be within an arm's length of Mark, or a brawl would arise. It was a pleasant change. For the first time, I felt like part of a "normal" family. Brent and I spent quality time going on road trips all over New Hampshire and Maine. My favorite drive was through the White Mountains, where we viewed the Old Man on the mountain before it collapsed. The drive offered the most breathtaking views.

Brent had always been an aviation enthusiast and introduced me to air shows, aviation museums, and spoke of his dream to become a private pilot himself. There was a boyish charm about him. He'd point and "ooh" and "ahh" whenever an airplane flew over, naming it with a glance. At thirty-three, Brent was fourteen years my senior, and I admired him for not giving up on his aspirations. I encouraged him to join a ground school, and that was it. He was on his way. His enthusiasm for aviation inspired me to start thinking about my destiny, but I loved working at the airline, so I was content for the moment. I focused my energy on my new relationship, and it felt like the beginning of something great.

Brent didn't know about my past, and I was okay with that. I tried to bury it deep and forget it ever happened. I wanted to focus on the future instead of dwelling on the remnants of my yesteryear. I waited a while before inviting Brent to my apartment because I still feared that Justin could show up unannounced. He hadn't come around in five months, but I always feared him. After a couple of nights of Brent visiting me, my fear came true when Brent found his tires slashed, so I had to tell him about Justin and his abuse.

Brent, being the defender he is, stepped up to protect me without hesitation. He lived with his brother and sister-in-law, Tommy and Sharon, and said I might be able to stay with them a while. I appreciated the thought but reassured him (and myself) that everything would be okay, but he persisted.

"I think you'd be safer living with me."

"I know, but I don't want to impose. I don't think it's necessary."

"It's not an imposition at all; I've already talked to Tommy and Sharon."

I sat there, speechless from the gesture. Then all the questions started.

"What will I do with my furniture?"

"We can sell it or put it in a storage facility."

I looked around my bare apartment, considering the idea. My friends handed down all my things. I only owned a light blue couch, twin bed, and my clothing.

"When do you want me to move in?"

"Right away. Let's stay here tonight and figure out what to do with your things later."

"Okay, I'll move in, but can we rent an apartment of our own soon?"

Brent agreed, so I packed my things, not knowing exactly where I was going. I felt nervous because I'd be meeting Tommy and Sharon for the first time, but Brent assured me we'd all get along great.

Tommy and Sharon were a down-to-earth couple who've been together for more than twenty years now. They welcomed me into their Kokopelli decorated apartment and made me feel at home. We spent most of our time laughing or watching movies. It was vastly different from any of my past relationships. Brent wasn't an alcoholic or drug addict, and I'd never heard him raise his voice. Tommy and Sharon had a loving relationship without domestic abuse. Theirs was the healthiest marriage I'd ever seen up until that point. It was my first experience with a relationship that didn't involve domestic violence, alcoholism, or abuse. It was a refreshing change.

Our new living arrangement was going great, and so was Brent's career. After years of working a demanding job, he got a well-deserved promotion and became Vice President of Maintenance. This position change made him my direct supervisor, which meant I needed to find another job due to the conflict of interest. It bummed me out because I loved my career as a maintenance planner, but my experience allowed me to stay within the industry, working at a commercial aircraft parts distribution company. I didn't earn as much money, but Brent's promotion allowed for the decrease in pay. After three months, we leased our apartment and started living together.

Brent and I moved to a small textile mill town in central New Hampshire. The move felt like an elevation in social status because, as embarrassing as it sounds, I'd have a dishwasher and microwave for the first time. I was proud because it was a place worthy of visitors. I thought about how proud Mama would be if she saw it and couldn't wait to invite her up for a visit. I hadn't seen her in a year, so I thought it was about time for her to meet Brent, because it felt like a lasting relationship. We had it all: a great apartment, financial stability, and a great connection with his family. I felt eager to take on my role as the woman of the house and looked to Brent to guide me. Luckily, he was the chef in the family because I never learned how to cook. He even enjoyed it. I didn't know how to be a "wife" or keep up with a house, so I relied on Brent to show me the way, and he did so happily. I looked forward to making friends with Brent's coworkers' wives, so they'd teach me how they did things. Brent was good to me, and I wanted to be the best girlfriend I could be for him. I was ready and willing to adapt to anything to make him happy. However, at twenty, I wasn't yet aware of how much I'd grow as a woman in the years to come.

CHAPTER TWELVE:
AFTEREFFECTS

About two years into my relationship with Brent, at the age of twenty-one, inner demons from my past started creeping up. I found myself withdrawing from the relationship, and I eventually shut down emotionally. Brent and I lived a perfect life. He was an earnest worker and a great provider. We had close friends that we spent time with on weekends and special occasions. Brent and I still went out on road trips and took the four-hour trek to Maine to visit his mom and dad whenever we could. I should have been happy, but I felt hollow, unfulfilled, and restless about our future. Brent checked off all the boxes, but I still felt something missing that I couldn't put my finger on. I thought I just needed a career change, so I left the aviation industry to give the tech world a try.

I became an assistant buyer at a telecom company and was thrilled about it. The career change came with a substantial pay increase, so surely the extra money would make me happier, I thought, and it did, for a while. I bought a new car, clothes, electronics, and furniture for our apartment, but loneliness still engulfed me.

Brent stayed the steadfast provider through it all, but I realized our relationship lacked fire and affection, and it left me vulnerable to temptation. The new job meant a lot of fresh faces and people to meet. I was a twenty-one-year-old young woman, yet I felt like an old hag. I refused many invitations from co-workers to go out after work. Not because I didn't want to go, but because I didn't know how to "be" around new people. I barely even knew myself.

Only one person could get through the barrier I'd put up, and that was Luke. Luke and I worked side by side in the same department. We worked the same schedule and had the same lunch hour, so we typically took our break together.

At the time, I told myself that being with a good man was more important than having passion between us. That was my first mistake. I discovered I'm a fiery person, and I don't do well if I feel stifled. Subconsciously, I sought out others to try to fill the void I'd had since I was a child. I wanted to feel loved and "special," giving me a false sense of worth.

They say you spend more time with co-workers than family, and that rang true for me. I confided in co-workers instead of Brent. That was my second mistake. Brent and I had trouble working on our problems because we didn't communicate about them. I desperately needed to be in therapy, but Brent and I didn't realize it at the time. Brent stood for stability more than love, and I wanted that to be enough for me. I thought it could be. But it wasn't. I was missing love and affection, and it left me vulnerable to perpetrators of all kinds.

Over four months, Luke and I grew to be close friends. We walked to lunch every workday and talked. He was the first platonic male friend I'd ever had who showed an interest in more than just going to bed with me. Our daily walks eventually progressed to meeting up with the rest of our co-workers after work. Brent worked second shift, so I was in no hurry to get home. The friendship with Luke stayed platonic until we both had a little too much to drink one evening. We arrived with a group of co-workers but ended up being the last two from our group to leave the bar. I ordered a glass of water and an appetizer to allow myself some time to sober up before driving home. Luke offered to stay with me. I told him he could share my food.

"No problem," he said with a chuckle.

Luke sat back down next to me and ordered himself water. He looked over at me, and I don't know what happened, but our eyes locked, and he leaned in to kiss me. The kiss was so emotional that I saw fireworks, and everything around us disappeared. The intensity of the encounter sobered me up, and by the time I realized what was happening, I was following him back to his place. I knew what I was doing was wrong, and I never would be able to fix breaking Brent's trust, but my desire for Luke washed away any chance of me changing my mind. We went straight to the bedroom when we got to his place, and I crossed the line. The power of the kiss was exhilarating, and it hooked me. It was the start of a very intense emotional relationship that I needed at the time. It was the one thing missing from my relationship with Brent. We cared for each other, but there were no fiery sparks between us in any way. Brent isn't incredibly romantic or affectionate. He's not lovey-dovey and rarely complimented me on my beauty or talents. I didn't feel loved by the man who claimed to be in love with me.

I kept my sexual relationship with Luke to myself. I sensed I was seeking attention and affection that I didn't get from Brent. I beat myself up for this for a long time, but now I understand my sexual traumas' aftereffects were driving my decisions. I was conflating sex with love and having the distorted belief that sex was all I offered in a relationship. Another reason I stepped outside the relationship.

Daddy didn't make me feel special, Mama didn't make me feel special, my extended family members didn't make me feel special, and now I didn't think I was unique or special to my boyfriend of two years. Brent didn't express a desire for me, so Luke's attraction to me gave me the illusion that I was "special" to him, and that was something I'd been searching for since I was a child. My motive was never to hurt Brent.

In June 2001, a couple of months after my relationship began with Luke, I started to feel torn and questioned whether we should move forward. I felt guilty after everything Brent did to take care of me and didn't think the affair with Luke would last. The fire burned bright, but it wasn't long before the flame started to flicker. The relationship was over by the end of the month, but we remained cordial. I made the decision to be with Brent and was looking forward to spending the long fourth of July weekend together. Before leaving the office, I donated blood to the Red Cross, drank my juice, ate my cookie, and headed out for the mall, where Brent and I planned to meet for dinner. We arrived around the same time and walked into the mall together.

"Hey there," Brent said as he reached out for a hug.

"Howdy," I replied with a smile and kiss on the cheek.

"Are you looking forward to dinner?"

"Oh, yeah, I donated blood, so I need something in my stomach."

"Perfect. Do you mind if we make one quick stop before?"

"Sure, lead the way."

Brent took my hand and led us through the mall past the food court and into a jewelry store. I didn't think anything of it until he described the jewelry he wanted to see.

"Welcome; what can I help you find today?"

"Engagement rings, please."

I spun around from a counter on the other side of the room and said, "WHAT?" We never discussed marriage before.

"Do you want to look?" Brent asked.

"Uh, yes, I want to look!" I responded.

The jeweler returned with several diamond styles for me to choose from. I fell in love with the emerald cut, so the jeweler brought out a couple of options. I felt nervous, holding an engagement ring in my hand. Especially knowing what I'd been up to the past few months. I started to feel guilty and queasy. Suddenly, the room began to spin, my face flushed, and I vomited all over the counter and passed out on the floor. A few minutes later, I opened my eyes to find Brent and three store associates surrounding me. I apologized immensely to the jewelry store staff and told them we'd be back. I felt so embarrassed walking through the mall. Brent and I ordered our dinner and took it home.

By Monday morning, I still felt horrible. I was queasy again and couldn't seem to hold down any food or water, so I made an appointment with my doctor. I went in for a routine checkup and urine sample. When the doctor came into the room, I expected to hear that I contracted a virus of some sort, but instead, I received a shock.

"Good news, I know why you passed out after donating blood."

"And?"

"Well, it appears that you're pregnant."

"Pregnant? I had no idea."

"Yes, ma'am, and based on your last menstrual, I'd say you're four to six weeks along."

"Are you sure?"

"We'll do a blood test to confirm, but the urine test is positive for pregnancy."

My mind started reeling. I added up the dates from when I was with Luke to see if there was an overlap. The times were so close that I didn't know who the father was. If I was six weeks pregnant, there was a possibility that Luke was the father, but if I were four weeks, then it would more likely be Brent's baby. My eyes started welling up with tears.

"What's wrong?" asked the doctor. "You're not happy about the results?"

"I'm confused. I'm not sure who the father is," I admitted.

The doctor came closer to me and put her hand on my knee. "Once we do the blood test, we'll have a better idea of your conception date. I'll be able to help you figure it out."

I asked when my due date might be, and she told me mid-to-late February. I just sat there, stunned. I'd gotten myself into a terrible predicament. The only way out of it was to be completely honest with Brent about my infidelity. He deserved to know that I might be carrying another man's child. The thirty-minute drive home from the doctor's office felt like an eternity. I knew Brent would be home when I got there. I took a deep breath before opening the door. Brent was on the computer in the bedroom.

"Hey, how did your appointment go?"

"It didn't go that great, actually," I said.

Brent turned his attention away from the computer to focus on me. "Why? What's wrong?" he asked.

"I'm pregnant," I uttered. But before Brent had the chance to react, I added, "and I don't know if you're the father."

Brent froze to process my confession.

"What do you mean? Whose baby could it be?"

"I was seeing another man for a couple of months, but it's over now."

I felt guilty about my infidelity. Brent's confusion turned to anger.

"How could you do this to me? How could you let this happen?"

"I'm so sorry this is hurting you. You deserve to know the truth, and I think the sooner, the better. We need to decide how we are going to move forward."

"If it's not my baby, what are you going to do?"

"If this baby isn't yours, it's still a part of me, and abortion isn't a possibility. Either we stay together and do this as a family, or we break up and go our separate ways."

"We just looked at rings together. I don't know what to do now. When will you know who the father is?"

"Well, I took a blood test that will give more exact information. But right now, you need to understand that this baby could still be yours. It's just that the dates are so close that I can't say for certain."

"When is your next doctor's appointment?"

"Next week."

"Can I go with you?"

"Of course. This way, you can ask the doctor anything you want."

The rest of the evening, I kept my distance from Brent. I genuinely hurt and surprised him with the news of my infidelity. The days leading up to the appointment were difficult. Brent could barely stand the sight of me. I just wanted to get to the truth, no matter what it was.

Of course, Brent wasn't the only person I needed to notify. Even though Luke and I officially ended things, he also had the right to know that he could potentially have a child on the way. I was nervous, and it was more difficult for me to give Luke the news than it had been for me to tell Brent. I went with the "Band-Aid" approach and just blurted it out. I arranged to meet Luke at the same bar where our affair began. We sat down at the bar. Luke ordered a beer, and I ordered a water.

"You're not drinking?" he asked.

"I'm pregnant, and it might be your baby," I blurted.

"What?" he asked with a laugh.

"I'm pregnant, and it might be your baby."

"You're not sure if it's my baby?"

"No, I'm not sure, but it may be yours."

Luke's reaction caught me by surprise. He was excited to hear the news.

"That's the best thing you've ever told me!" he said while giving me a big hug. "Give me all the details. When are you due? Is it a boy or a girl?"

The barrage of questions overwhelmed me.

"Woah, woah, woah, let's not get ahead of ourselves. I'm not sure if the baby is yours yet."

"I think it is," he proclaimed. "I can just feel it."

I didn't know what to do. Luke was so excited where Brent felt betrayed. If the baby was Luke's, I wondered if I should be with him instead. Are Luke and I supposed to be together? If he's not the father, he'd be so disappointed. The questions kept scrolling through my mind, but I remained neutral until I knew for sure.

"Don't get too excited. Please. Just in case," I continued.

"Okay, okay, I'll wait until after your appointment."

On the day of my appointment, Brent and I ate breakfast together before driving to the doctor's office. He barely spoke two words to me the entire time, and I didn't blame him. I just gave him the space he needed. He sat next to me in the doctor's office, but he couldn't have been further away from me mentally or emotionally. He just needed to hear the news before deciding what to do. We both needed that. Finally, they called my name, and we headed back to the room. Dr. Lemay introduced herself to Brent.

"How are you?" she asked him.

"I'll tell you after we talk about this test," he nervously joked.

"I do understand that." Dr. Lemay looked at me. "Do I have your permission to speak openly?"

"Yes, you do."

She continued. "Okay, then. Based on your lab results, you're not as far along as I thought, so you have a new due date. I'd say the chances are greater that Brent is the father."

"Really?" Brent exclaimed.

"Yes." She smiled. "Your new due date is March 1st."

Brent and I hugged each other, and I cried. I shed tears knowing that Brent was relieved, but I cried tears of sadness, too, for Luke. He'd been so genuinely happy to hear the news that I knew he'd be disappointed. I dreaded making the call to him. During the ride home, Brent and I talked about the future of our relationship.

"Where do we go from here?" Brent asked.

"Well, I'd like to make things work if we can. Now that we know you're the father of our baby, we can move on and forget any of this ever happened. Can't we?" I asked.

"I'd like that," Brent responded. "But I need to know that you're faithful to me."

"I know. I promise I won't do it again. It was just a moment of weakness that I won't repeat."

And I believed that at the time. I felt so relieved that the news came out in Brent's favor that I wanted to give our relationship more effort. I promised Brent and myself that I'd gotten everything out of my system and was ready to be a mom.

Luke and I still worked together, so I tried to be extra delicate with him. We still had to work side by side, no matter what happened. I called him up the next morning.

"Hi, do you have a minute?" I asked.

"Of course, I always have a minute for you."

He always said cute things like that to me. It only made it more difficult to hurt him.

"I have news, but it's not good," I said. "The doctor said she thinks Brent is the father. I'm not as far along as she thought, so my new due date is March 1st. I'm sorry it isn't the news you wanted to hear."

"Me too," he said somberly. "I don't want to hear from you anymore."

"I understand, but we have to work together, so I'd like to keep it civil between us."

"Just don't speak to me, and we'll be fine." And then he hung up.

The situation was surely going to make things uncomfortable for me at work, so I knew I'd have to get another job. I just didn't realize it would be so soon.

CHAPTER THIRTEEN:
MEMORY AND EMOTIONAL
SUPPRESSION

The following weekend, Brent and I went on our usual expedition through Maine, stopping in to visit with his mom and dad for a few hours before taking the four-hour ride back to New Hampshire. Brent wanted to surprise them with our news about the pregnancy. It felt a little too premature, so I felt wary, but Brent's excitement convinced me to let him share the news.

"What are you guys doing here?" asked Anne. "You didn't tell us you were coming up this weekend."

"We decided to surprise you," Brent told her, as he wrapped her up in a big hug.

"You lucked out because your dad happens to be over for dinner."

Anne opened the front door to her single-wide trailer. "John, look who's here!"

Brent's dad greeted us with hugs and asked why we didn't call.

"We were in the area and just thought we'd stop by," Brent told them.

"In the area? Aren't you about four hours outside of your area?" joked his mom.

"Well, yes, but we come with special news," Brent teased.

"What news?" asked his mom.

"Well, why don't you and Daddy sit down for this."

I sat at the table with John and Anne while Brent shared the news.

"We're pregnant!" Brent exclaimed.

"Pregnant?" shouted his mother.

"Are you kidding me?" asked his dad.

"Yes, pregnant, and no, we're not kidding," he laughed as they all surrounded me for a group hug.

"But that's not all," he said.

I turned to him. "What do you mean, that's not all? Do you know something I don't?" I asked with a chuckle.

"Kind of," he responded with a grin.

I turned to tell his parents that I had no idea what he was talking about, and when I turned back, Brent was on his knee in front of me holding a ring.

"Oh, my God! What is this?" I asked.

Brent's parents started crying. "This is the happiest day of our lives," his mom said.

Brent joked, "I haven't asked her yet!"

He then turned back to me. "Will you marry me?"

I was in shock because I never expected a proposal so soon after admitting that I'd cheated on him. I thought a marriage proposal would be the last thing on his mind. It was the last thing on mine, and I didn't know what to say. My first reaction was to say no, but I didn't have it in me to do that after seeing the happiness on his parents' faces.

"Yes! Of course, I will," I eventually said.

We engaged in a group hug to celebrate the moment. Brent's parents cried tears of joy. They couldn't wait for the baby to be born, and now we had a wedding to plan. We spent the next couple of hours laughing about how our spontaneous road trips were going to end and how our lives would change forever. Changes that Brent and I confidently said we were ready to make. Brent was thirty-six, and I just turned twenty-two. It felt like our life was moving in the right direction. We continued to work and prepare for our first baby to arrive, but not everything was smooth in my life.

The following Monday morning, I went into a company meeting, donning my new engagement ring. I intended to keep it private, but my coworker announced it in our morning meeting in front of a group of about twenty of my peers, including Luke.

"Congratulations are in order because Yvonne got engaged over the weekend!"

Luke was sitting directly across from me and darted his eyes toward mine and mouthed, "WOW," at the news. Broadcast of the engagement only made our working relationship worse. When word got out that I was pregnant, rumors churned about my relationship with Luke and my work environment became onerous. Our coworkers took sides, and all fell on team Luke. Luke's tenure with the company was much longer than mine, so many of them were his personal friends. It didn't matter, though, because just two short months later, we received word that our company would be laying people off, and my position was in jeopardy. A few days later, my supervisor called me into the office to give me the news that he'd cut my position. I was four months pregnant and concerned about not having healthcare. I no longer had a job. Luke kept his job and his friendships with his coworkers, while everyone turned against me.

When Brent found out, he suggested I stay home for the rest of the pregnancy. I felt excited about the opportunity. I'd use the chance to get ready for the baby and plan our wedding. We chose to get married after the baby was born, in April 2002, only six short

145

months away. Planning our wedding brought on some unexpected challenges. The first was that we didn't have money saved and had to plan a wedding for fifty on a budget. We underestimated how difficult it would be planning for a baby and wedding simultaneously.

Another dilemma emerged when it was time to put together the guest list. Mama was the first person to know of our engagement, and the first thing she said was, "I hope your dad isn't coming." I didn't want to discuss it with her, but I thought about asking my dad to walk me down the aisle. Every girl wants their daddy on their wedding day, and I was no different. I ignored the comment for the moment. It wasn't worth getting into a conversation over. I convinced her she'd be busy with the baby and not to worry. We wanted our wedding day to be a celebration of love and an introduction to our new child. It was a big day for everyone. Mama warned me ahead of time that many family members wouldn't be able to make the trip to New Hampshire, so I prepared myself for a small showing.

Six months before the wedding, I made it official with my dad by inviting him to walk me down the aisle. He seemed more excited than I expected him to be, which put me at ease. He promised to be on his best behavior, and I planned to hold him to it.

I also learned that only two others from my family would be making the wedding, Mama and Aunt Melody. I felt disappointed but tried to understand and again looked for the unseen benefit. "Eh, it's for the best. The fewer family members interacting with Daddy, the better," I told myself.

Meanwhile, I continued nesting at the apartment and preparing for the baby, while Brent worked to support the family. We were grateful for his job security because it seemed like we bought something new for the baby every weekend. By the new year, we stocked up with a natural wood crib that we set up in our bedroom, onesies, multiple packs of diapers, and a top-of-the-line stroller and car seat. Now it was time to wait. March 1st came and went, and still no baby. Before we knew it, I was twelve days past my due date, so doctors scheduled an induction. We chose March 14th, 2002 because it was my mom's birthday. It would be a great birthday present for her since she planned to be in town for the birth. Mama flew in on the ninth of March to help me get ready for the big day. She helped me pack a bag and told me a few things to expect during labor. She reminded me how she was alone when I was born and expressed happiness that Brent would be by my side.

"Just think, you're days away from having a baby!" Mama said.

"I KNOW!" I shrieked with excitement, kissed her, and went to bed.

I woke up around 4 a.m. on March 11 with early contractions. By six in the morning, contractions got stronger and closer together. We called the doctor, and she told us to come in right away, so we loaded our things and drove to the hospital. After we settled into the room, I changed out of my clothes and into a hospital gown. My contractions were painful but bearable. Unfortunately for me, giving birth wouldn't be an easy feat. I labored for a total of thirty-six-and-a-half hours, and had a tough time delivering. I pushed for over two hours with no luck. The last half hour was the worst. The epidural wore off, and I felt everything.

I finally heard the nurse say, "Give it one final push," and I pushed with all my might. At 3:22 p.m. on March 13th, our older daughter, Ashley, was born, and our lives changed forever.

Brent and I were thrilled to have a little girl and decided against a paternity test. She looked perfect, except for her conehead from her long journey through my birth canal. The nurses kept commenting about how long her neck was and about her "big brown eyes" when babies are usually born with grey or blue eyes. They transformed into the most beautiful hazel green. She was the light of our life, and I knew I'd never let anything happen to her. Now that Ashley was in the world, we couldn't wait to show her off to everyone at our wedding in six weeks.

The final months leading up to the wedding were the most stressful. I underrated the amount of work it takes to plan even the smallest wedding. It requires all the same vendors, and everyone knows going through the proposal process can be the most time-consuming task to complete. We didn't expect anything extravagant, but we wanted it to be beautiful. At the time, I wanted to marry Brent because it was the right thing to do. We weren't in love, but now we had Ashley and tried to give her the best life. I was eager to have stability in my life and knew he would provide it. I later learned that Brent also had doubts about getting married but moved forward for the same reasons I did. We had a child now, and it was the best thing for her. It became clear after Ashley was born that Brent and I wouldn't be able to reignite our spark, but at the time, I thought I'd be able to live without expressed love, affection, and passion because my needs weren't the priority. Ashley needed my love, support, and attention. I didn't want to let her down. A week before the wedding, I received a call from Mama with information that could ruin everything.

"I'm sorry, but I'm calling with sad news," she told me after we'd said our hellos.

"What happened? Are Granny and Pawpaw okay?"

"Yes, everyone here is fine. It's your dad."

"What happened?"

"Your dad drank himself into the hospital. He has alcohol poisoning and probably won't be able to make the wedding next week."

"Well, I'm used to being let down by him, so I guess I'm not surprised."

"Well, it gets worse."

"What do you mean?"

"Your dad has ripped the IV out of his arm a couple of times trying to escape the hospital, so he's being restrained and will go to jail for assaulting a doctor when he's healthier."

The message didn't faze me. By this time, I was so emotionally numb from Daddy's disappointments that I brushed it off like it meant nothing. I was almost relieved because he wouldn't be able to get drunk and embarrass me, but not surprised. It's like I already expected he wouldn't make it. He let me down so many times that I'd have been more shocked if he showed up.

"Well, you know what that means, Mom?"

"What, honey?"

"Will you walk me down the aisle?"

"You know I will, but have you thought about asking Mark?"

"I've thought about it and decided not to invite him."

"Okay, that's up to you. I'd be happy to walk you."

Mama and Aunt Melody arrived a few days before the wedding to help with last-minute errands and spend time with the baby. Everything on the morning of the wedding seemed surreal. It didn't feel like my wedding day. I felt exhausted after being up with Ashley the night before. I nursed, so she was always close. We opted for a morning wedding, so I'd only have a couple of hours to get myself and Ashley ready. It was a beautiful sunny day, but chilly for April. I dressed Ashley in an adorable off-white, lacy dress and bundled her up for the ride to the ceremony. Brent arranged for a white limo to bring me, Mama, and Aunt Melody to the venue.

"Are you getting excited now?" Aunt Melody asked.

"I'm not feeling excited. It feels like any other day to me. I wish we waited a little longer."

"Well, you can't change anything now, so just try to make the best of it," Mama counseled.

"I know, I just thought I'd feel differently on my wedding day. I don't feel like a bride."

Deep down, I knew I was questioning it all, but there was no turning back now. We were on our way to the chapel, and I was getting married. I chalked my lack of excitement up to hormones and lack of sleep. I hoped things would be different when I got there.

When we pulled up to the venue, I stepped out of the limo to a photographer snapping my photo. My white satin, strapless ballgown with silver embroidery wasn't the dress of my dreams. I bought it sight unseen from a wedding catalog. The skirt had so much volume that it was difficult to get in and out of the limo.

As I appeared from the vehicle, I quietly questioned my choice to hire a photographer. I didn't feel beautiful and thought it was a waste of money. When I caught a glimpse of the wedding guests waiting, I convinced myself it was a waste. Some of our guests hadn't dressed for a wedding. They wore jeans, flannel shirts, T-shirts, and shorts. It was embarrassing but out of my control. It felt like no one was taking our wedding seriously, and I thought that's because I wasn't taking it seriously either.

Nothing about the day felt romantic or remarkable, but I blamed myself for that. Nobody wants to drink and dance at ten in the morning. I just wanted the event to end. When it was time to walk, Mama was by my side in a beautiful red suit. I felt nervous walking in front of our friends and family, so I focused on Brent waiting at the altar. He looked worried and unsure of himself, but the ceremony went ahead without a hitch.

It didn't feel like a celebration at all. There was a celebratory toast of champagne, but I didn't partake. No one else bought beer from the bar or danced at the reception, and the place cleared out by noon. Brent and I packed up our few gifts and headed back to the apartment. We didn't go on a honeymoon because Brent wanted to save every penny for Ashley. I respected him so much for that since my parents never sacrificed that way for me. It made sense to me, so I didn't complain.

The first downfall of our marriage was getting married for the wrong reasons to begin with. Then it seemed like Brent started viewing me as "Mommy" instead of "Yvonne." After we got married, we stopped going on road trips or romantic dates. Our lives completely revolved around our daughter, and we stopped nurturing each other as a couple. I slowly tried to adjust to married life. Brent continued working while I stayed home to care for Ashley.

Being a new mom brought me into a new circle of stay-at-home moms, and I finally made a few friends. My severe social anxiety still held me back many days, but I made it onto all the Pampered Chef, Tupperware, jewelry, and candle party invite lists. I wasn't a fan of those parties, but it felt nice that the group of moms included me. Each one tried to sucker me into selling whatever product they pitched.

I gave the Tupperware thing a try for a while, but my lack of social circle made booking parties difficult. Besides, Brent kept a close eye on the purse strings and felt it was all a waste of money. He viewed start-up costs as a waste, not an investment. At the time, I appreciated the way he protected the money in our accounts because it allowed us to save up to buy our first home, a charming two-bedroom split-level ranch near Crystal Lake in New Hampshire. Again, we had it all. Our own home, a beautiful two-year-old daughter, new cars, and a golden retriever we called Winchester.

The only thing missing was the white picket fence and my sense of purpose. Yes, I loved being with Ashley, but I missed daily adult interaction after two years and began feeling the pull to work outside the home again. This time, I didn't just want a job; I wanted a career. That opportunity came in early 2004 when Ashley was about two years old, by way of an offer to work at a well-known home and auto insurance company. I found the position in the classified section of our local newspaper. The ad grabbed me because the company offered to supply the testing material and pay for the state test after six months of on-the-job training. If I passed the test, I'd be a licensed home and auto insurance representative in the state of New Hampshire and could focus on growing a distinguished career in a new industry.

I was never interested in the insurance industry, but it was an opportunity to gain experience in new things. So, with Brent's support, I accepted the position and agreed to start as soon as I arranged childcare, which took about a week. I adapted well to my new professional role quickly but struggled to fit in with my co-workers. It was a family-run business, so some co-workers didn't care for newcomers. I believed at the time that everything happens for a reason, so I didn't feel anxious or upset when, within three months, Brent and I found out we were pregnant with our second child, due in December 2004.

This time, we opted to know the gender and discovered we'd have a second girl. My second pregnancy was a lot less stressful since paternity was never in question, but sadly, I don't remember much about the pregnancy itself. I believe at the time, aftereffects were starting to creep up, so I dissociated much of the time. My biggest regret is that my dissociation may have wiped my memory of that special time in my life. I don't remember the day I found out I was pregnant or have memories of my growing belly.

I worked at the insurance agency throughout and focused hard on studying for the New Hampshire insurance license. My goal was to hang in long enough to take the test and get it over with before the new baby arrived. I wonder now if my drive to get back to work was a way to distract myself from thoughts that were starting to haunt me. I had the financial stability I always dreamed of, but not the emotional support I needed to properly address my past. Fortunately, despite the madness going on in my head, I was able to stay on track, and six weeks before the birth of our second child, I took and passed the state test. I'd be able to use the license anywhere in the state. I looked forward to finding a position at a different agency after my pregnancy leave. But first, we needed to finish getting ready for our new daughter.

I suspect this is when self-sabotage started rearing her ugly head. According to https://www.psychologytoday.com/us/basics /self-sabotage, self-sabotage is having thoughts or behavior patterns that hold you back or prevent you from doing the things you want to do. Self-sabotage can be anything from procrastination to putting yourself in situations that could disrupt the uncomfortable feeling of comfort.

For me, I self-sabotaged by not committing to my relationship with Brent. After everything that happened with Ashely, I expected he would grow to resent me and eventually leave me. I didn't have the emotional security that I needed. I didn't have the security of affection or reassurance I needed within my marriage. I was emotionally vulnerable and the repetitive compulsion to seek out that emotional connection and affection in other places started spooling up.

Having a second daughter made preparation much easier this time around. We already had everything we needed, but we officially outgrew our little two-bedroom ranch. We wanted to start searching for house number two, but not before welcoming our beautiful daughter, Claire, to our family in December 2004. Within a year, we found a beautiful three-bedroom beige colonial home with dark green shutters that rested on an acre of land in central New Hampshire and closed on the property in August 2005. It was perfect for our growing family.

After the move, I felt a pull to continue my education. Brent supported the decision and agreed to take care of the girls while I attended classes. I was excited to start and enrolled in state college in 2006 at the age of twenty-seven. I felt optimistic about the new beginning and looked forward to growing from the experience. Thinking back, it's possible my eagerness to return to school at that time of my life was just another attempt to distract myself from the pain I was feeling. I thought the financial stability with Brent was enough to sustain me, but I was still deeply unhappy. I didn't yet realize the unhappiness was stemming from my past. Convinced I "overcame," I tucked all the uncomfortable memories down as far as I could. I was successful in keeping them tucked away for a while.

I worked full-time while attending classes and was eventually invited to stay after class so one of my professors could tutor me. Little did I know this decision would lead to a rabbit hole of emotional triggers, dark manipulation, and at times, mind control.

His name was Craig, and I didn't know what I was getting myself into with him. This man infiltrated my life and nearly destroyed me. My first impression of him was positive. He used his sense of humor throughout class and our tutoring sessions, which made our discussions more enjoyable. Craig seemed like a normal human being. He turned out to be the cruelest, most sadistic, and bizarre person I've ever known. Craig was about eighteen years my senior, overweight, balding, unassuming, unattractive, yet charismatic, and my professor. One night during class I raised my hand to ask a question.

"Yes, Yvette?" he asked.

"What did you call me?" I replied jokingly.

Craig stopped writing on the notepad in his lap, turned toward me, and apologized for the mistake with a blush. "My apologies for that; I meant Yvonne."

I asked my question, and for the next few months, Craig called me Yvette as a joke. I was flattered to have a running joke with the professor. Sometimes he'd tell me, "You're ninety-nine percent Yvonne and only one percent of Yvette today." I didn't inquire further about what his statement meant, I just smiled and continued my day. I soon learned it was Craig's calculated way of building rapport to groom me for an inappropriate relationship. I'm convinced he sensed my vulnerability and made me his target.

About three months into the semester, some students stayed behind to further discuss the lesson, so I joined them. At the end of the night, I was the last to leave the building, so Craig offered to walk me to my car. During the short walk to the parking lot, he struck up an odd conversation that caught me off guard. It felt strange because I expected Craig to be virtuous as a professor. I soon learned this guy had no boundaries or morals at all. It was the first time we were ever alone.

"Are you married?" he asked.

"Yes, I am, with two daughters. How about you?"

"My wife and I are separated. I'm living with my brother right now," he offered.

"Oh, I'm sorry to hear that."

"Thanks. She's disabled, so things have been a challenge."

"May I ask how she's disabled?"

"She's afflicted with several illnesses."

"I'm sorry to hear that. I hope your wife feels better."

"There's no cure. I left because I just couldn't do it anymore."

"Do what?"

"Take care of her every need."

I thought it was sad that he didn't want to take care of his wife. "Well, I'm sure everything will work out the way it's supposed to."

"How's the 'sizzle' in your marriage?" he asked.

The question took me aback, but I answered honestly since he had been candid with me.

"It lacks fire, but we're both focused on our children, so it works for us."

Finally, we reached our vehicles. I thanked Craig for the chaperone and told him I'd see him at the next class.

That conversation was Craig's way to test my emotional availability and evaluate the status of my marriage. I recognized it because it was a tactic I'd used. Whenever I'd meet a married/taken man I was interested in, I'd test their loyalty with a simple question, "Tell me about your wife/girlfriend." If they answered with "Eh, it's okay," or "Eh, *insert negative connotation here*," I'd see it as an "opening" to push a little further. I'd probe them to see how far they'd go. I wanted to know if they would cross the line for me or keep their loyalty to their partner. The reality is, I just wanted someone to love, need, and want me. I wanted to be special to someone. Since no one held boundaries with me as a child, I didn't expect it to be any different as an adult.

On the ride home, I wished I hadn't been so personal about my relationship with Brent. He was a good guy, took care of our family, and supported my return to school. Still, the feeling that something was "missing" between us kept getting stronger. At the time, I didn't have intentions to go outside the marriage. I resigned myself to stay faithful to Brent, but I never really felt married. I never felt "taken" or "spoken for," even though technically I was. I was bound to him because of my label as his wife, not because my husband made me feel that way.

Still, he was family-oriented, and I respected him immensely. He gave me a stable life for the first time, even if there was no romantic connection between us. We became Mommy and Daddy and forgot about Brent and Yvonne, hoping that Mommy and Daddy would be enough. We didn't marry for love, so we doomed our marriage from the start. Without love, there can be no trust, and without trust, there's no foundation, and without a foundation, our union came crashing down. I put the conversation with my professor out of my mind by the time I got home and continued the evening as usual. Brent and I got the girls into bed and sat down to watch television for the evening.

The following week, Craig offered up his phone number to the class and requested our information in return so he would know who was calling or emailing. I gave mine, as did the rest of the class. The next morning, an email from Craig was waiting for me:

"I've met many beautiful, smart, and funny women, but never a woman who possessed all those qualities at once."

At the time, the compliment was flattering, but it surprised me. Now I understand that type of communication between a professor and student is inappropriate and the start of the grooming process. Craig crossed the ethical boundary the day he sent that email to me, but his follow-up emails proved to be equally complimentary, poetic, and as thoughtful as the last (and inappropriate). I didn't know how to feel. He made himself romantically and emotionally available to me and that made me feel important. It was something I'd never felt before. His infatuation with me was flattering. He doted on me more than anyone ever had, all with his words, and I quickly fell under his spell.

He was the initiator of the emails, and it felt exhilarating. Even though I didn't find him physically attractive, his position of power and status at the college turned me on. He created an environment within our "friendship" to obsess over each other, and he expected it. He pulled me in by insisting that we stay in contact throughout the day and night, every day of the week. If he called, I answered. If he emailed, I responded right away, and he agreed to give me the same attention.

In the beginning, he stayed true to his word, and I replied to him right away, knowing he'd reciprocate. If I didn't answer right away, he'd send multiple emails about how he "missed" me and couldn't "wait to see your name in my inbox." His words flattered me, and each one left me wanting more. Sporadic messages turned into daily "good morning" emails, which escalated to multiple email conversations throughout the day. We stayed connected as designed, emailing continuously throughout the day, and chatting online at night.

We kept our emotional affair a secret from everyone at the college, knowing the administration wouldn't take kindly to a professor fraternizing with a student. Craig was a risk taker and couldn't help himself. He liked to walk the room during class and discreetly run his fingers across my back as he walked behind me and soon, progressed to nightly video chats. It wasn't long before Craig suggested we meet away from the college at a local park for lunch the following day. I agreed and looked forward to it. It had been a busy week at the office, so it would be nice to step away for an hour at lunchtime.

The following day, I was nervous for my lunch hour to roll around. Something didn't feel right about meeting with Craig, but I ignored my intuition like so many times before. When I arrived at the park, Craig was there waiting.

"Shall we go somewhere for lunch or take a walk?" he asked.

"Let's go for a walk," I decided.

As we walked, Craig asked questions about my marriage and my childhood. He paid attention to insignificant details about me and gained my trust. He could read me like a book, knowing when to push for more information and precisely when to back off. I didn't reveal my past to many people, so I was apprehensive. He assured me my secrets were safe with him and said he'd been hiding a few secrets of his own. I believed him. As I revealed the details about my past to Craig, I felt liberated. Free from the burden of silence. Brent didn't know some of the things I shared with Craig. I felt honored that he was interested in me. He was intelligent, successful, and respectful. I felt special.

A few months into our communication, Craig invited me to have lunch with him again, but this time at his second job. He also held a prestigious position at a major corporation, and it was just ten minutes from my office. Craig instructed me to park and meet him in front of the building. I parked and checked my makeup in the mirror. I sat in the car until I saw him come out of the building. I hopped out and nervously walked up to the entrance. Craig welcomed me with a hug and escorted me through the building and to his office, introducing me to coworkers along the way.

"What's for lunch?" I asked, hoping to shake my nerves.

At the time, I mistook my nerves for desire and my fear for excitement. I thought I wanted Craig to be interested in me, but now I know it was fear all along. I was afraid Craig would make a move on me, and I didn't want it to happen. It's a feeling I'm now familiar with because I recognize it as part of what drives my repetition compulsions.

"I made us salads, is that okay?"

"Sure, sounds great. Where shall we eat?"

"We're going to hang out in my office."

"Okie dokie," I said.

Finally, we turned down a corridor, and Craig pointed to a door. "Here we are."

. He stopped in the doorway of the office adjacent to his for a brief conversation before we disappeared into his office, and he closed the door behind us. It was smaller than I expected and cluttered with manuals, stuffed animals, and paperwork. There was a small window that faced the woods in the back of the building. Craig pulled the cord on a small lamp, and a dim light cast across his wood desk.

"Nice office. Where should I sit?"

"You can sit anywhere you want."

I chose an office chair away from his desk and nervously made small talk. "How long have you worked here?"

"It seems like forever, but it's only been fifteen years."

"Wow. Do you see yourself retiring here?"

"I don't know, we'll see. I don't have to worry about that for a while."

I nervously ate my salad in between small talk as coworkers buzzed right outside of his office. Afterward, I stood up to throw away my salad container, and that's when Craig waylaid me, pushed me against the wall and started kissing me. It shocked me, but I didn't rebuff him. I was in auto-pilot mode and went along with it even though I didn't want it. I never expected him to make a move with so many people around.

I felt emotionally numb and trapped. Craig told me that everyone just went into a meeting, so we were alone. I felt flustered, but trepidation stopped me from rejecting his advances. I didn't want to anger him or have him deny me. I felt blindsided. *Did I lead him on? Did I give a sign that it was okay for him to do this?* My internal battle churned as he continued to take things further and pulled my skirt up above my waist.

Our emails were flirtatious but not sexual, so he caught me off-guard. I felt weak and powerless to stop it. Again, it felt like sex was all I had to offer. I wondered what it would be like to be with him, but not there. Not like that. I imagined it to be more meaningful, but it wasn't. Craig continued to yank my panties down and entered me from behind. The encounter was rape thinly veiled as passion. He was in a position of power, and he took advantage of me. He didn't ask for my consent; he just attacked me. It was over within a few minutes, and at that moment, our relationship shifted from professor and student to confidante and lover, or more accurately; abuser and victim.

After a couple of months of loving interactions, Craig alluded to having a mysterious side. Being the psychologically curious person I am, it intrigued me, and I wanted to know more. As he did with me, I assured him that there was nothing he could say that would affect our relationship. Before now, we'd spent time together at local motels, and I slept in his marital bed while his wife was away for a weekend. He made me feel loved, wanted, and needed. When he asked about my upbringing, I was candid about my hardships, so with everything I'd been through in my life, I was sure I'd seen it all, heard it all, and experienced it all, but I learned much more than I expected.

Craig divulged that he was interested in BDSM, which is bondage and discipline, consisting of physical or psychological restraints, domination, and submission, involving an exchange of power and control, sadism, and masochism, which refers to taking pleasure in others' or one's pain or humiliation. He started the conversation by showing me photos of people in bondage. Most were your typical men in restraints, with women standing over them holding a whip. It felt like healthy sexual exploration at the time, so I obliged. I was willing to role-play if that was what he wanted. He knew I'd do anything to make him happy.

I soon came to understand that this fetish went much deeper than innocent role-playing. As time went on, the images and links became more sadistic, and some were downright disturbing. Everything about our relationship changed. We started treading uncharted territory for me, but I wanted to prove I was up for the challenge. Craig repeatedly assured me that this shift in sexual appetite wouldn't affect our loving bond, but he lied. Our relationship unexpectedly shifted from a warm, nurturing, and thoughtful arrangement to a secret, sinister, alternative lifestyle. As he continued revealing more of himself to me, I found the skeletons in his closet to be much more profound than mine. He was careful not to unveil the darkest secret of them all.

Unbeknownst to me, Brent discovered my affair with Craig early on after becoming suspicious of my sudden late-night internet use. He secretly installed a tracking program on my computer. Brent intercepted every email, every online chat conversation, and every internet search I did. He continued to track me for months before I found out when he confronted me with an email he intercepted. Brent caught me red-handed, and I faced the truth. There wasn't a confrontation, really, just an acknowledgment that he had stacks of evidence against Craig and me.

"I have every single communication exchange between the two of you," admitted Brent. "What if I put them all in an envelope and mail it to his wife?" Brent threatened.

"He's separated from his wife," I retorted.

"How about if I send them to his job then?" he calmly suggested.

"Brent, please, you don't have to take it that far. It's not worth it. I'll end it," I falsely promised.

Brent's threat to expose Craig if I continued the relationship wasn't enough for me to end it. Craig had no idea that Brent knew about us. I didn't tell him because I was afraid he'd break things off with me out of fear for his career. Instead, I somehow convinced Brent that it wasn't worth destroying Craig's career over, and he agreed not to mail the evidence. I was again codependent in an unhealthy relationship, and my fear of abandonment blinded my view of reality. I continued to spend time with Craig during the week and communicate with him on Yahoo! messenger at night.

I think deep down, Brent knew I wouldn't end it, and he was right. I was all-in with Craig. We started talking about life together, and he gave me the false hope that we would be together someday. He told me he loved me more than he ever loved his wife and wanted to grow old with me. He said everything I wanted to hear from a romantic partner, and it roped me in, clenching my devotion to him.

I fell madly in love with Craig's words. Finally, someone loved me as much as I loved them, and we expressed it in similar ways. Even though Brent was aware of my transgression, the "I don't give a fuck" switch in my brain turned on, and nothing else mattered but the relationship with Craig. I suddenly felt inhibited in my marriage, and I wanted to bust out to transform into this new person that Craig was creating me to be. I thought he was breathing life into me, but he sucked it out of me instead.

My marriage to Brent was on the rocks, but Brent's career was going exceedingly well. He was going places in the aviation industry and offered a once-in-a-lifetime opportunity to head up the maintenance department for a Florida-based airline. Brent couldn't pass up the opportunity, even though it meant he'd have to move to Florida right away. Within weeks, the life we knew had turned upside down. Brent packed up and made his way to sunny Florida. There wasn't a discussion of divorce or separation, so we were still very much together. The plan was for him to move ahead of the girls and me to get situated and find a place to live. His absence meant that I'd have to juggle a full-time job and take care of a two- and four-year-old on my own. It was challenging for me but gave me a taste of freedom.

I continued my affair with Craig while Brent was away, but Brent had a watchful eye on me. He put up with it because, deep down, he hoped things would get better once everyone reunited in Florida. Although times got hard, staying in New Hampshire was never a choice. Our daughters needed their father, so I was committed to following him anywhere his career would take him. Few people worked as hard as Brent did to achieve his goals, and I wasn't going to get in his way. Once we decided, we put our plan into motion by enlisting the help of a realtor to sell our home.

The girls and I were stuck in New Hampshire until we sold the house. In the meantime, Brent stayed in Florida during the week and flew home on the weekends whenever possible. For the next ten months, I spent every waking hour of free time online with Craig.

CHAPTER FOURTEEN:
MIND CONTROL

I continued receiving salacious pornography links from Craig. Each one became increasingly more disgusting, perverted, and violent. He emailed so many throughout the day that it was hard to keep up. I didn't know how he managed to get any work done as much as he surfed the internet.

Craig was, by far, the most complex and disturbing human being I have ever met in my life, and that was saying a lot coming from me. He attended church every week and claimed to be a devout Christian. He was living a double (or triple) life. He was a regular churchgoer, professional, and college professor during the day and a sadomasochist at night. It was difficult to reconcile his religious beliefs with his sexual desires. I equated it to my family's so-called "Christianity" and their penchant for forgiving child molesters.

Craig just had a way of getting away with things. He somehow kept his perversions concealed from his wife for twenty-five years.

According to Craig, his wife was clueless about his desires and believed him to be an honest and faithful husband. She questioned him one time when she found a BDSM-inspired comic in his briefcase. He brushed it off by saying it was a gag gift from a coworker, and she bought it. He kept his sexual deviancy concealed for their entire marriage. He told me there were quite a few women before me. His journey to the "dark" side, he said, began during his engagement, and he successfully eluded suspicion while having affairs throughout the marriage. I was fascinated by his ability to keep it all under a veil of secrecy. If what he said was true, his wife had been sleeping next to a stranger for years.

Pornography links became more extreme, increasingly violent, and included even more disgusting humiliation methods than before. It confused me. My thoughts became diluted with brutal images of whippings, human toilets, and sadistic humiliation involving bestiality. But this paled in comparison to his real desire, which he finally revealed to me.

He wanted to be "cucked." A cuckold is a man in a relationship with an unfaithful wife or girlfriend. Craig wanted me to have relations with other men, specifically well-endowed Black men, while he watched. I struggled to grasp how he could wish for this while claiming to love me. It was hard to believe him, but my need for him blinded me. I tried to impress him; I wanted to understand.

The violent, bloody links turned into images of well-endowed Black men with white women. His search terms morphed from "interracial relationship" to "extreme humiliation." These videos equally shocked me. Some included men engaged in forced fellatio and sodomy. In contrast, others focused on the humiliation of forcing the husband to clean the wife's lovers' semen from her body with their tongue.

I pressed him on why this type of relationship interested him, but his explanation was never clear. It was more confusing than revealing. He said he hated the videos. He hated the images. He hated the thought of me with someone else. It made no sense to me and wasn't what I wanted. His fetishes kept getting stranger and stranger. He wanted me to humiliate him for his small penis even though his lack of endowment never bothered me. He also asked me to kick him in the testicles on more than one occasion. It was incomprehensible to me.

Just when things couldn't get weirder, Craig started sending videos of himself masturbating from all over the place. From work, while on vacation with his wife, in public bathroom stalls, and from inside a glory hole booth he often frequented. He would engage in glory hole play with other patrons and send photos and videos of his acts. He even liked to walk around for days with items inserted into his anus. He'd wear an air cast on his leg to disguise the new limp in his walk. He vehemently denied having bisexual or gay tendencies, which made things more confusing for me. How could someone without those tendencies have the desire to do these bizarre things with people of the same sex?

I wanted to end the relationship, but figuring Craig out became my compulsion. My self-esteem didn't exist. Craig repeatedly told me that no one would love me as much as he did, and I believed it. He fully controlled my mind. He manipulated my behavior by using my emotions against me. Craig would get mad at me for being "too nice" to him if I were loving. When I tried to be assertive toward him, he'd become irate until I'd cower back, needing extra reassurance from him that everything was okay. He controlled me by withholding those assurances and used my fear of abandonment against me until I caved and did whatever he wanted me to do.

I was in constant "panic" mode with him. If he sent an email, I'd respond within minutes. If I didn't, I'd get an email asserting that I wasn't attentive enough, and he'd threaten to cut off all communications, which was one of the things I hated the most. He sensed my fear of abandonment and preyed on it. Within a year and a half, our once-loving relationship was now a full-blown psychological ordeal. Craig was always taking things to the next level. Within weeks of revealing his new fetish, he wanted our BDSM fantasy to become a reality.

Craig tried to arrange meetings with like-minded men for discreet dominant sex. He assured me it was what he wanted (or didn't want?). He promised he'd be by my side the whole way, but that was just another lie. Still, I felt compelled to stay true to my word. There was nothing more important than doing what I said I was going to do. Let down so many times throughout my life, I was resolute to conquer this new way of life. I promised unconditional love, and I was going to come through.

These recollections are some of my darkest days and worst memories. Craig wanted to meet strangers (Black men) for sex while he was humiliated in every possible way. I hated the thought of watching him doing it, but I wanted to make him happy. Not surprisingly, nothing he did ever made him happy. Nothing I did was ever good enough for him, and I knew I made a mistake when I agreed to his plan.

Craig immediately took to the internet to find him a "suitable" mate. He scoured chat rooms and Craigslist for men willing to take part in his sick games of domination and humiliation. He only searched for a few minutes before finding a man that could meet that same day. He arranged for us to meet the stranger at a local restaurant within two hours of contact. The meeting's purpose was to make sure Craig and I felt "safe," though I don't think it would've mattered either way. Now, I can't help but wonder how he found someone so quickly. In hindsight, I wonder if he knew this "stranger" all along? I was sick to my stomach. I didn't want to do this. I loved Craig and had no interest in watching these strangers humiliate and whip him, but he said it was what he wanted, and my support of it would prove my love for him.

I parked at the back of the restaurant. It was a cold, snowy day. I contemplated backing out, but there was no turning back. Craig went ahead of us to arrange everything, and the ramifications of messing it up sent me into a panic. I checked myself in the mirror and touched up my red lipstick before making my way to the entrance. It was lunchtime, so the restaurant was bustling. As instructed, I walked in and found one-person fitting Craig's description, a man wearing a red polo shirt. He was an average guy, in his forties, attractive and tall. I walked over to him.

"Are you waiting for someone?"

"Yes, I am. Are you Yvonne?"

"Yes. Nice to meet you. What's your name?"

"Are you hungry?"

"Not really but thank you."

I didn't know this man's name, but here we were plotting a sexcapade together.

"Have you ever done this?" he asked.

"No, this is my first time. How about you?" My heart pounded through my chest and the knot in my stomach got tighter.

"I've only met one other man this way. It went well, so I thought I'd try it again. I'm intrigued that your boyfriend is so into it."

"He's the only reason I'm here."

"You must love him very much."

"You could say that," I responded.

Then the stranger told me what he prearranged with Craig. "Craig arranged a room for us at the hotel up the street," he said. "Once we get to the room, Craig will already be waiting."

My stomach fell to my feet. I expected to walk in with Craig and wondered why he changed the plan, although it didn't matter because the entire situation was out of my control anyway.

"Okay, now what?" I asked.

"If you're ready, just follow me. Are you ready?"

"I'm ready," I answered.

But I wasn't. I felt distraught and called Craig as soon as I got into my car.

"Hi, we're leaving the restaurant now."

"Hi, good. Do you know what to do?"

"Um, well, he told me you're there waiting, so I'm not sure."

"Just do what I say. You're not in charge."

"I know, but I don't know if we can trust this stranger."

"Do you want to do this or not?" Craig barked. "Because if you don't, I can call the whole thing off, and you'll never hear from me again. Is that what you want?"

"No, of course not; I just want to make sure this is really what you want."

"Yvonne, this is more than what I want. You're making me the happiest man by supporting this for me. You're making my dream come true."

I'd never say no to that, and he knew it. I felt a renewed sense of purpose as I followed behind the stranger but felt increasingly uncomfortable about what could happen. I'd never done anything like this before and had no idea how things would go. As I sat outside the hotel, waiting for the stranger to get out of the car, I reached out to Craig one final time, hoping he'd change his mind and tell me to forget it.

"Are you sure you want this?" I asked.

"If you ask me again, I'm canceling it all, and you have proven you're not the woman I thought you are."

"No, no, no. I'm going to do this for you. You can believe in me."

"I love you very much for doing this."

I still had reservations but did as he told me, even though I didn't get excited about the sexual acts Craig wanted to perform. The stranger and I entered the motel through the side door and took the stairs up to the second floor to room 212. The latch propped the door open about two inches. I opened the door with bated breath, not knowing what I was going to find on the other side. I rubbed my sweaty palms down the side of my skirt as the door opened. I didn't see Craig until I stepped further into the room. He was almost nude, wearing only a leather vest and leather mask.

"I'm ready for you, master," Craig said to the stranger.

"What's your name?" I asked the man again.

"I agreed to no names."

I sat in the armchair next to the window, unsure of what would come next. We were at a sleazy, one-star hotel, and I wondered how many times Craig had been there before me. As I waited, I thought about the stranger and how his demeanor was hard to read. I didn't know what to expect from him. I felt a familiar knot in my stomach, telling me I didn't want to go through with this, but my mind took over, and I tried to make sense out of nonsense. I convinced myself to go through with it because it was what Craig wanted. Again, I put someone else's needs above my own. Abusers groomed me for this throughout the years. I cringed when the stranger began laying out his "tools" for the event, which included a whip, restraints, clothespins, rubber bands, and a paddle. I must have dissociated because I don't remember every aspect of the event. I just recall checking in with Craig again, after it all ended.

"Craig, are you happy I did as you asked? I'm glad that's over."

"You're right. It's over. I can't be with someone that would allow someone to do this to me," Craig threatened.

I'd never felt more confused than I did at that moment. I did precisely what this man wanted and even "checked in" multiple times to make sure, and now he was leaving me? I did this for him, and he was breaking up with me? Craig yelled obscenities at me until I broke down in tears. I didn't know what to do, so I quickly gathered my things to leave the room. The stranger was visibly uncomfortable with the unexpected drama and left the room before Craig could get his shoes on.

I tried to call Craig from the car, but he ignored my calls. I sent emails that went unanswered as well. I was sure the relationship we had was over, and I felt abandoned all over again. Craig's sociopathic behavior was beyond comprehension. He spent weeks building me up to do this, and now he was ending the relationship over it. He put me high on a pedestal, only to watch me come crashing down. After giving me the silent treatment for a week, Craig agreed to stay in the relationship, but new sadistic behavior became the trend. The loving, caring exchanges were long gone and replaced with dark, sadistic bargaining tactics instead. He wanted me to be nasty to him and would get angry if I wasn't vile enough toward him and accused me of "not having it in me." The truth is, he was right. I didn't have it in me.

I'm a lover, not a fighter. I still tried to give Craig what he wanted, but nothing was ever good enough. He suggested other arrangements after a while, and I cringed, knowing how the last one ended. I hated it but didn't have a choice. I lost all self-esteem and all sense of self-worth. This man swept me off my feet with loving words, only to send me crashing to the ground. He lied to me and manipulated me. I thought he loved and cherished me, but he used and abused me instead.

Because Brent lived in Florida, the girls stayed in daycare during the day, so that's when I tried to spend time with Craig. Instead, Craig made and then sabotaged all other arrangements, then blamed me for their downfall to keep control over me. He'd refuse to cooperate with agreed terms, or he'd criticize me for doing what he asked me to do. Cruelty became the norm, and even though I wanted to end the relationship, I felt deeply dependent on our daily conversations. At the time, a day without an email from him felt like torture to me. He controlled my mind and emotions.

He convinced me he was genuinely in love with me, and this was his way of showing it. It was easy to convince myself that he cared about me because being in a confused state of mind and deep pain wasn't new for me. He made me feel I deserved the cruel treatment, and I believed him. It had been this way my whole life. I found that to be just how life was.

After ten months and with all these things whirling in my mind, I prepared for the move south to Florida. Our house sold, so it was time for the girls and me to reunite with Brent. Craig didn't seem to care that I was moving out of state. He declined multiple opportunities to spend time together despite the time crunch. He suddenly had no time for me and no longer got right back to me if I reached out. I knew the relationship would never work long distance, but I desperately tried to hold on. My fear of abandonment kicked in, and I decided to do everything to "fix" whatever I did wrong to cause his changed behavior.

I tried to connect with Craig before the move to strengthen our bond, and he rejected me. Now I only had a few weeks to reconcile the relationship. I'd fallen head over heels in love with my warped professor and dreaded being away from him. It wasn't the relationship I wanted, but I promised him that he could trust me, and I didn't want to let him down.

The day before we moved, I received an email from Craig vowing to keep our relationship going long distance and rededicated himself to email and Skype communication. Part of me wanted things to get better between Brent and me after moving to Florida for our girls' sake, but our marriage took a turn for the worse. At the time, I thought I'd manage both relationships effectively. Brent stayed with me for the kids. He rarely showed his jealousy, which reinforced my belief that he didn't love me. The only other thing holding him back was funds to hire an attorney. It was bad enough that I continued an online relationship with Craig, but other problems began coming out of the woodwork.

I expressed my desire for a loving relationship, but the passion he'd once complimented me for had become my weakness in his eyes. He'd say I didn't have it in me to do the things he wanted. I wanted to prove him wrong, and he knew it. He worked reverse psychology like an expert. He knew if he said I "couldn't" do something, I'd try twice as hard to do it. Not because I wanted to prove him wrong, but because that's who I am. I rise to challenges because that's all I know to do. It took me a long time to realize that I'm not bound to rise to any challenge I don't want to take on.

One of my favorite quotes from Maya Angelou says, "When someone shows you who they are, believe them the first time." I've heard this repeated by Oprah, Dr. Phil, and others, and over time, in my experience, it has proven right. I didn't want to believe I wasn't the person for Craig. He wanted me to be cruel, angry, violent, openly unfaithful, and treat him poorly—all things I wasn't capable of being. I tried to be someone I wasn't to please him. He said I wasn't capable of being the person he needed, and I didn't have it in me to admit that he was right. Now, I'm proud I'm not the woman he wanted me to be, and I finally see him for who he is, a manipulative sexual predator with more-than-serious psychological issues.

Brent was willing to forgive me, but how could he love me after everything I'd done to him? What was it going to take for him to walk away? This was new to me. What kind of a man stands by a woman like me? A good man, that's who—a man who can put his children before himself and their happiness above his hurt feelings. But even the most celebrated men have a breaking point.

Brent's breaking point came about seven years into our marriage when we learned that Luke is, in fact, Ashley's biological father. The older Ashley got, the more she resembled Luke. Her eyes and nose are undeniably his. At the time, Ashley was being tested due to developmental delay, so I ordered an at home DNA test to know for sure. It was imperative to have her full medical history. After the truth came out, Brent just couldn't take it anymore, and in 2010, he officially filed for divorce. We tried to stay together for the kids, the money, and its convenience, but it wasn't salvageable, and divorce became the only choice. Brent had grown angry and cold toward me, which was entirely understandable. Craig spent two years convincing me that no one cared about me more than he did, and I believed him.

When Luke learned the news about Ashley, he was shocked. He never pursued me for paternity reasons, because why would he? He didn't believe he was the father and neither did I. I was wrong and so was my doctor. That realization really shook me and caused me to spin a little out of control with guilt. Not only did Luke miss seven years of Ashley's life, but so did his parents, who wanted nothing more than to be the best loving grandparents they could be.

Luke and his parents were thrilled to hear the news and anxiously awaited permission to travel from New Hampshire to Florida to meet their daughter and granddaughter. I supported the meeting because Ashley had the right to know who her biological family is. Conversely, the news crushed Brent, and he didn't find it proper to introduce everyone so soon. It was an incredibly challenging time for our family. My guilt over the seven years Luke and his family lost with Ashley was a big driving force in my desire for them to meet. They already missed so much that it wouldn't be fair to make them wait any longer to get to know each other. I agreed to the meeting against Brent's wishes and arranged it for the following month. Brent knew it was happening and did not approve at all. I think this action against his wishes sealed the deal on our fate.

The divorce papers came in June 2010, seven months after our relocation to Florida. I didn't contest. Who could blame Brent for wanting to divorce me? I felt sad for my girls but relieved for myself and Brent. Frankly, I expected him to divorce me sooner, and I wanted him to. After some months of going back and forth with attorneys, we agreed to go to mediation. Mediation was one of our most stressful days, but we went into the meeting united, with our daughters' best interests at heart.

Brent and I found out we're better friends than spouses. We had rough times, no doubt, but we always set that aside for the girls. Our mission was to do everything in our power to make sure the divorce didn't negatively affect the girls. We are the best co-parents we can be. He'd keep the girls when I worked the second shift, and I'd keep them with me when he left the state for weeks on end for training. He was there when I needed him, and I was there for him. We had each other and counted on it. After the divorce, I didn't tell Brent I stayed in contact with Craig, and I stayed out of his personal life, although I hoped he'd meet someone he deserved. He deserved so much more than I gave him.

On October 14, 2010, Brent and I met at his attorney's office to sign our divorce papers. Despite the sadness of the day, we found ways to lighten the mood. We went to lunch together as we waited for the final documents to be prepared and joked about splitting the check. We stayed in good spirits knowing that we did what was in our children's best interests. We wanted the girls to grow up with happy, healthy parents, not parents who fought all the time.

It was a hard meeting, but after an hour or so, we agreed and ended things amicably. Brent remained Ashley's legal father and has continued coparenting with me. Luke sees Ashley several times a year and despite all the drama, the three of us have managed to keep a great relationship. Thankfully, he and his family hold no animosity toward me, and I remain close with his mom. Both of my girls are incredibly lucky to have them in their life. They've received cards for every holiday and birthday ever since. Although this enormous obstacle was behind us, substantial changes were still ahead.

It had been over a year since I'd had active employment. I wanted the time to get the girls settled in and communicate with Craig. When Craig learned about the divorce, he pulled back from me even further. He realized the dissolution of my marriage put him in the hot seat. He'd fantasized with me for years about how it would be "if we both were divorced," but I don't think he ever expected me to become available. I never expected him to ever divorce his wife.

Brent and I still lived together in our two-level family townhouse after the divorce, but it was time for me to find my own place. I was juggling some incredibly stressful situations but needed to focus on life after my marriage with Brent. I needed to find a job and a place to live right away, so I focused on finding an apartment within the girl's school district and making sure the girls were settling in okay.

I was lucky to find full-time employment at a beautiful hotel and resort. I felt blessed that the girls attended the best schools in the state, and in April 2010, I leased a two-bedroom, two-bath apartment with a lovely balcony for the girls and me. It was the first time I lived on my own since 1999, and I looked forward to it. Even though our marriage was over, and through everything I'd done to him, Brent and I kept our friendship. I expected him to hate me, but he doesn't. Brent loves his daughters and would never leave their side.

Craig and I stayed in communication during all these transitions, but I was growing frustrated with our relationship. We were a thousand miles apart, and I hoped he'd revert to the loving relationship we'd started with, but it never happened. We somehow managed to see each other a couple of times after my divorce. Each time, I hoped and expressed the need for a regular visit, but Craig would start an argument about it. He wanted me to come prepared to watch a strange man dominate, humiliate, and sodomize him. I wanted to love him. Any time I'd express a need for loving affection, he'd accuse me of not loving him. It always ended with him being cruel to me and me begging for his forgiveness. He owned me, and he knew it. He took full advantage of me while he could.

You'd think I'd be happy to be away from him, but I needed him more than ever. In my twenties, I was exploring my sexuality. I used my body to get affection. I needed to feel loved. My self-esteem was down in the dumps with my self-worth. The girls were young, and I felt guilty out of fear that I abandoned them the way my mom abandoned me. I told myself that I wasn't there for them. I left them with their father to give me time to have affairs and destroyed our family. I was too hard on myself. I understand now I didn't abandon my children. Their father took care of them. I came home every night, fed them breakfast, lunch, and dinner every day, and showered them with hugs and kisses all the time. Yes, I made mistakes, but I didn't abandon my girls. I never put them in danger, and they are trauma-free to this day (aside from our divorce).

I didn't see the distinction until recently and have since relinquished years of guilt as a result. I've come to realize that the level of abuse and neglect I endured as a child was tragic and entirely preventable. I watch over my girls and monitor their behavior. I'm mindful of movie ratings and their friends. They have rules and structure in their lives. They don't go near strangers or hang out with friends without my permission. These are all things that would have made an immense difference in my life as a child.

***

Craig continued abusing his power and exploiting my vulnerabilities. The definition of emotional transference is the redirection of desires, feelings, and expectations from one person and applying them to another person. Craig made me believe I was the most important person in his world, that he couldn't get enough of me, and initially told me he loved me. I transferred my emotional expectations from Brent to Craig, clinging to my desperate need to feel "special" to someone. Unfortunately, sex was the only thing that made me feel that way because it was the only time I felt "special" as a child. My parents' lack of attention made me thirsty for attention from anyone that showed the slightest interest in me.

CHAPTER FIFTEEN:
ANXIETY

Despite my failed personal life, I was excelling professionally. I'd been at the gorgeous, 500-room, brand-name resort since 2010. I started in food and beverage and loved it. It's where I met my best friend, Sue, and got to collaborate with great people who made work fun. It kept my mind off the craziness that was my life. No one knew about my relationship with Craig, and I kept it that way. Instead, I focused on several growth opportunities within my first year. Turning my focus back to my career gave me the distraction I needed away from Craig.

I quickly climbed the corporate ladder and received my first internal promotion by the summer of 2011. Management recognized me for my efforts at the quarterly awards ceremony and gave me my first-ever accolade, a Service Star, in October of 2011. The acknowledgment solidified my desire to continue growing my career within the hospitality industry. At this time, I set my sights on the sales department, where I'd be able to productively use my people skills and contribute directly to the company's success.

Things started deteriorating at the resort in the fall of 2011, and by September 2012, our hotel would be under a new, independent management company. I didn't take the news well. It felt like I was in the middle of a nasty divorce. All employees felt respected, valued, and cared about by management. We didn't know what to expect with the new management company or even know who they were until they came in for orientation.

My livelihood was in jeopardy. The new incoming managers showed no respect to tenured team members, and it kept everyone on edge, especially me. During the transition, upper management assured everyone that it would be "business as usual"; however, everything changed. The new management team didn't know me from Adam's house cat, so I'd have to prove myself all over again, and I didn't know if I was up for the challenge. I'd spent many quality hours with upper management expressing my desire to be in sales, and they mentored me to reach that goal. It felt like I had to start all over, and that challenge was incredibly daunting to me.

I blamed stress and the toxic atmosphere at work for my anxiety, which provoked a depression fed by a deep well of anger turned inward. I felt used, unappreciated, and unimportant. These emotions activated overwhelming, unwanted memories and flashbacks that hammered on me day and night.

Human Resources reassured us that we could reapply for our same positions at the same pay rate but couldn't guarantee everyone would keep their jobs. The announcement came with more unwelcome news. Most of the remaining executive committee from the previous management company were also leaving, and new members were coming in. Many of the directors had been with the company for many years and transferred to other properties. Most of my mentors were leaving, and I took it personally.

It was a loss for me, and I grieved deeply for everyone leaving. It was like a family ripping apart, which triggered my fear of abandonment. These managers knew my work ethic, accomplishments, and higher potential. They supported my goals and promised to help me reach them. Their replacements were strangers, and I'd have to prove myself all over again.

From the beginning, I intended to be a group sales manager at the resort, so I stayed focused on my goal. Sales managers booked corporate and social events and had a direct impact on the property's success. It was one of the highest-paying positions with a base salary plus commissions—not to mention upper management's respect. The newest members of the "team" enjoyed drama and stirred the pot whenever they could. They'd talk behind my back and smile at my face. By September 2012, the hotel chain I was so proud to work for, was no more. We were under new management and the atmosphere greatly changed.

Craig and I remained in constant contact throughout all the turmoil at the resort. I turned to him for comfort but found none. I felt emotionally and mentally exhausted. Craig's obsession with fetish porn was in overdrive. He continued sending link after link until four a.m. some nights and expected me to watch every single one. Sometimes, he'd send them all night long, leaving only an hour or two of sleep. He controlled my rest with masturbation. If I fell asleep, he'd end the video call and go silent for days or weeks at a time, which felt torturous for me.

By 2012, Craig and I crossed the five-year mark since our relationship began, and he kept complete control over me. He expected me to tell him what I was doing every moment of the day. He insisted I inform him about every appointment, meeting, lunch with friends, or if I invited a guest to my home. Craig made me set my Skype settings to answer automatically, so he could call in and "check" on me anytime he wanted. I always left the computer on and logged in to Skype. Of course, he didn't do the same for me. By this time, he made me beg before he'd turn his camera on for me. He'd disappear from communication for hours at a time and get angry at me if I asked about his whereabouts, but he'd go off the deep end if I did the same to him. The double standard felt maddening, and Craig kept digging his heels in further and further.

I became increasingly miserable and emotionally poisoned with mind control.

When Craig was communicating with me, he'd force me to stay awake until he was ready to pleasure himself. I found a way to function on minimal sleep, but the darkness overwhelmed me, and I fell into a deep depression for years. I grew sick of the way Craig treated me and people taking advantage of me at the resort. I knew it was time to walk away from Craig when his obsession took another disturbing turn. He began sending images of younger-looking girls. He insisted they were at least eighteen and just had "childlike" bodies.

He spoke of wanting young girls to mistreat him like the women did in the videos he sent. He suggested mothers should train their girls on how to be dominant and be cruel to men. He wanted to live in a dungeon like a slave. He said he fantasized about having stepdaughters he could watch grow up and train to bring their boyfriends home for sex and force him to watch. He said it would be a "punishment" for him, not "enjoyable."

This revelation made my stomach turn. I thought of my two daughters and wanted nothing to do with his newest fantasy. He crossed the line. That's all it took to open my eyes. It was my opportunity to do things differently than my mom and I did. I'd never put them in harm's way or allow a pervert to exploit them. I'd no longer communicate with him now that I knew what his deepest, darkest secret was. I suddenly realized how deranged he and his ideas were, and I wanted out of his sick fantasy world. It wasn't a drawn-out or dramatic process. I just stopped emailing one day, and that was the end of him. I closed all accounts associated with him and erased him from my life. I was thankful to be free from the mental prison I was in for five years, but now I was contending with the distorted image of love he portrayed. I needed to learn how to love myself. I'd have to fight to regain my self-worth, confidence, and self-esteem. I had a long road ahead.

After I ghosted Craig, I met up with Sue to watch the final *Twilight* movie. During the movie, the characters' display of love for one another deeply touched me. After the movie, I sat in the car with Sue and told her all about my horrible experience with Craig. I wiped my tear-soaked cheeks and proclaimed to Sue that I longed to find someone to love me with that type of loyalty and intensity. Remarkably, I met Gavin just three days later in October 2012, and my life started to change.

By January 2013, Gavin and I were deeply in love and things were looking up at the resort. One of the sales assistants received a promotion, so they sought a replacement. I applied right away and got the job. The promotion came with a four-dollar-per-hour pay raise and a set Monday through Friday schedule. I was through with the second shift and could be home with the girls at night. I achieved my goal of reaching the sales department. This achievement was a great start, and I felt incredibly thankful. But I knew I'd eventually need to make more money. I'd wait patiently for a sales manager position to open, and then I'd make my move. I didn't want to be in that two-bedroom apartment forever.

In November 2013, I approached my director about stepping into the sales manager role with a heartfelt letter expressing why I thought I was best for the job. I didn't have sales experience within the industry but was enthusiastic about the will to succeed. And if given a chance, my knowledge of the resort would prove to be enough. To my delight, my director granted an interview for the next day. I was incredibly nervous but confident in my ability. I knew I was the right person for the job.

The following morning, I chose to wear the only business attire I owned, a black skirt and white blouse. I hoped that our HR Director, Mia, would see me in a different light and not just as the menial worker I was at the time. During the interview, I presented contracts that I executed on behalf of the company. I offered page after page of professional relationships I'd built in my role as assistant. I pressed that I'd be an asset if they'd give me the opportunity.

At the end of my presentation, I sat quietly and admired the view of luscious property grounds from her window as she reviewed the documents I'd given her. I admired her awards and reiterated my love for the resort. Photos of employees covered her walls. After a few minutes, she dropped the documents on top of her desk and looked back at me with a smile.

"Okay, Yvonne. I have everything I need to make my decision. Thanks for coming in."

Walking back to my office, I agonized that the other candidates looked better than me on paper, but thankfully, Mia didn't make me wait long, calling me only a few hours later. I saw her name on my caller ID, and it felt like my heart was going to jump out of my chest. I wanted this more than anything and didn't know if rejection would break me. My palms were sweaty as I answered the phone.

"Can you come back to my office for a moment?" Mia asked.

"Sure! I'm on my way." I raced back, hoping it was going to be good news.

"Come on in," I heard Mia say from the other side.

I took a deep breath and walked in. I'd never been more nervous. I just wanted it to be over. Mia motioned for me to sit in the chair across from her. "I asked you to come back because we've reached a decision."

The anticipation was killing me, so I blurted out, "What's the verdict?"

"We are offering you the sales manager position."

I didn't contain my excitement, and I jumped up to thank her and gave her a big hug. I finally had the schedule I needed, and the salary increase I deserved. In a matter of three years, I transformed from wearing a server uniform to designer dresses.

***

My first year as a manager was a tremendous success. I turned contracts consistently and outperformed the more seasoned sales managers on the team. When the sales director said we were short on cash flow, I got a client to pay $50K in advance. When he asked for more business out of the West Coast, I delivered. When the sales director said he wanted an airline or cruise line crew to contract with us, I brought them a contract for the largest cruise line crew the property had ever won. My confidence soared. I'd proven that whatever management needed, I'd be able to get the job done.

When my salary review came a year later, I was sure I'd done enough to prove my worth. But management denied it. Instead, the administration increased my share of work by assigning me all small markets (a full-time job) and significant markets for the West Coast, Southwest, and Midwest (another full-time position), but that wasn't all. They also made me the interim marketing information coordinator, which required a full-time person to manage properly.

I became responsible for three full-time positions, tripling my responsibility with the amount of territory they assigned to me, but not my compensation. Sure, the potential commission would be lucrative, but my base pay didn't change. However, their expectations of me did. The new administration took advantage of my ambition by assigning me the most extensive sales territory, yet they paid me the least. My performance exceeded their expectations, but they still didn't pay me fairly.

In early 2014, well on my way to having a banner year in sales, not only did I learn the owners had grown unhappy with the new management team and our property was on the market again, but my dad suffered a stroke which landed him in a rehabilitative hospital. I wanted to visit, but I didn't know if I could handle seeing him after all these years. All the while, I convinced myself that I was okay. Thankfully, Gavin stood by my side through it all. He endured my anxiety attacks and long hours. He's the only person to ever *show* me what true love is all about. He didn't just tell me he loved me. He proved it (even though I didn't ask him to) when he stood by me during those stressful days at the resort. I knew my search for love was over when Gavin proposed to me in March 2014, and we set our wedding date one year to the day of our engagement in March 2015.

CHAPTER SIXTEEN:
WEDDING STRESS

In January 2015, our wedding was two months away and it became more challenging to be in the office. My stress was so high that I lost twenty pounds in two weeks, and it became more challenging to manage my emotions. I lost any filter I may have had and began snapping at my director and other coworkers. It became so bad that I eventually arranged to work from home several days a week. I felt devastated. Sales managers, catering, and the directors were all exhausted and bitter, and it showed. I felt like management was sabotaging my success. I gave my all to prove I was an asset to the company. And even though the demanding work did pay off and I exceeded my goal, I started to believe upper management didn't think I deserved the success I was getting.

In February 2015, I turned in $500K worth of signed contracts for management approval. I spent months collaborating with the executive team and my director to get the terms where we wanted them. But when it came time for the client to sign, my director forced me to retract my contract with no other explanation. I later found out that management knew the property was transitioning and stopped accepting contracts to sabotage the new management company. My paranoia didn't arise from a conspiracy theory that I created on my own. An Executive Committee member confirmed it.

I found myself at a crossroads. I had the choice to tough it out with the incoming management company or walk away from a professional goal I'd spent five years working to reach. I didn't know which way I should go. I wasn't sure if I even had a choice. I put so much pressure on myself to keep going, but all these stressors contributed to my "breakdown" during that call with my mom in February 2015. Gavin made it clear he supported my decision to leave work to focus on therapy full time, but I wasn't ready to do that yet. We still had a wedding to pay for, and it was fast approaching. Gavin and I agreed to wait until after the wedding to make that decision, which was only a month away.

When our wedding weekend rolled around a month later, I felt utterly exhausted from spending time with family and friends I hadn't seen in such a long time. This time, my mom, Granny, aunt, her husband, and my best cousin, attended. I even invited Mark to stand in for the father/daughter dance. During the ceremony, there wasn't a dry eye in the crowd. Everyone there felt our sincerity, and it became clear that Gavin and I cherished each other. When our officiant spoke those special words, Gavin and I sealed the deal with our trademark relationship agreement high-five and a kiss.

At this moment, any negativity drained from my body, and I felt nothing but immense joy and happiness. During the reception, I looked around for two of my closest work colleagues, but they were absent. Marge was there (as a guest of another co-worker) and gleefully informed me that they weren't in attendance to make a statement over a rumor they heard.

When I asked what it was about, she said, "Oh, now's not a good time."

Gavin and I looked at each other, perplexed. "You mean now's not the right time to talk about what you already brought up? Okay."

It annoyed me she said anything at all. Gavin and I continued making our rounds to thank everyone for coming. It did hurt me that my so-called friends used our wedding to make a statement. Again, people I trusted and respected didn't reciprocate that friendship. The kicker is the rumor was all a big lie Marge started! It hurt me deeply that they didn't even give me the courtesy of a phone call to get my side of the story. Their actions also hurt Gavin, but truthfully, none of that mattered that day, because I still felt beautiful, I felt loved, and I felt worthy for the first time in my life. That's when my newest journey began.

Immediately following the honeymoon in April 2015, I struggled hard to stay motivated. At work, we began hearing rumors that the resort was on the market yet again. Marge was the source of the leaks too and continuously talked about the hotel's dire financial situation. I didn't understand how that was possible with all the business our sales team brought in. There wasn't recognition of our success, only demands for more, and we did as they asked. One colleague booked an airline crew, and another scheduled sizeable religious groups, while I brought in groups from various other markets. *How was all this never enough?*

The previous three months had been a whirlwind for me. I got married in March, went on a honeymoon in April, made the final decision to end my successful sales career in May, and was in therapy by June 2015.

On May 8, 2015, ironically, the same date as Uncle Marty's murder seventeen years earlier, I killed my sales career. I drove to the hotel for the last time, knowing I'd never return. It was a painful decision to make, but I had no choice at all. I typed up my resignation, effective immediately, and went straight to the director, Juan, who was sitting in his office.

"Do you have a minute?"

"Sure, come on in."

We positioned ourselves at the small conference table overlooking the well-manicured property. I took a deep breath before speaking.

"After much consideration, I've decided today will be my final day at the resort."

"I'm shocked to hear this news, Yvonne. We were prepared to give you a promotion and a raise."

"As much as I appreciate your confidence in me, I need to take care of my mental health and I can't do that while working full time."

"What if we offer sixty-five thousand per year and the next twenty days off to regroup?"

"That's very generous, but I just can't do it."

Juan let out an audible sigh as he flipped his tie over his shoulder. "Yvonne, we really need you."

"I appreciate that, but I have to do this for myself."

An offer of $65,000 a year ($20K salary increase) and the next twenty days off to regroup wasn't enough for me to stay. I left behind literally one million dollars' worth of signed contracts, which already put me over my annual quota halfway through the year. Paychecks, including bonuses, would flow in the rest of the year, but I had to give it all up for my sanity, and this was when the healing process began for me. I started my sessions with Laura about a month later.

***

I'd been in therapy with Laura for about a month when I broached the subject of visiting my dad. I felt a pull to him ever since he had his stroke a year earlier.

"I think I want to go visit my dad."

"Do you think you're ready for that?"

"I don't know, but I'm afraid he's going to die, and I want the girls to meet him."

Laura was apprehensive, but ultimately supported my decision to go. Gavin and I drove to Alabama to visit my dad for the first time in about fifteen years. I wanted my daughters to meet their grandfather, and it felt safe because he was in the controlled environment of a hospital. It felt like I was meeting my dad for the first time. Although I was anxious about the "what ifs," I knew Gavin would never let anything happen to any of us.

My entire body trembled as we approached the hospital. I didn't know what to expect when I saw Dad. After we parked, Gavin took a moment to check in with me.

"How are you feeling? Are you ready to do this?"

"I think I'm as ready as I'm ever going to be."

I took a couple of deep breaths, "Okay, let's go do this."

The four of us hopped out of our navy-blue SUV we nicknamed "Superman" and stretched our bodies from the long drive.

"Are you girls ready to meet your grandpa?" Gavin asked to break the tension.

"Yeah!" the girls declared happily.

At the time, I didn't know if I wanted an ongoing relationship with my dad. He'd previously neglected to acknowledge his abuse, only excusing it by blaming the other party, including my mom. For now, I decided to just focus on the visit in front of me and introducing him to his granddaughters.

The main entrance opened to a huge common area with patients meandering about. An elderly receptionist greeted us as we entered.

"Welcome. Who are you here to visit today?"

I told her my dad's name and she directed us to his room where he was waiting for us to arrive. My heart pounded as we walked down the long hallway. He saw us before we saw him.

"I'm in here, Eve. Get in here and give me a hug!"

I peered in the next room and there he was, sitting in his lounge chair. We hurried in and greeted him with hugs.

"Hi Dad! It's so good to see you! And these are your granddaughters, Ashley and Claire."

"Oh, I can't believe how big ya'll have gotten! Come give me a hug."

The girls smiled and leaned down for a hug. I snapped a photo with my phone.

"There. It's official! I have it on record. You've finally met."

Daddy smiled ear to ear. I could tell he was happy to see us all.

"What do you want to do today?"

"Whatever you want. I'd love to take a drive to get something to eat."

"Sounds good to me, are you ready to go?"

"I sure am. I've been waiting all morning for this."

We gathered Dad's medication and walking cane and made our way out of the small hospital room. It was strange to see my dad so feeble, but I felt safer. My biggest fear was that he'd ask to stop at the liquor store, but thankfully, he eased my concerns during the trudge down the endless hallway.

"Do you know I haven't had a drink in years?"

"I didn't know that. That's great news! I'm really proud of you, Dad."

The head nurse posted at the nurse's station saw us approaching.

"I see your daughter finally made it. You must be excited to get out of here for a while?"

"I sure am! It's the first time I've been out in months. I finally get to eat some *real* food."

The nurse smiled back at him. "Can I come with you?" and the two shared a laugh.

It was nice to hear my dad laugh. I don't know that I even knew what it sounded like until that moment.

"Do I need to have him back by a certain time?"

"Yes, please make sure he's back by 5:00 p.m. for dinner. If he's not here, he'll miss it."

And with that, we made our way out of the hospital and into the warm, Alabama summer breeze. During our road trip, Daddy brought us down memory lane showing Gavin and the girls places we lived in the past. Since we were on the topic of our past, I decided to ask him some questions.

"Dad, do you know all the things I went through as a child?"

"No, baby girl, I'm sorry to say that I don't."

And he's probably right because he was absent the entire time. I pushed a little more.

"Do you remember all the domestic violence I've seen?"

"I remember, but nobody knows what I put up with from your mom."

There it was. The victim blaming, I was so conditioned to hear.

I could only muster up three words in response, "Oh, I'm sure."

My fear of my dad came rushing back. I stopped short of prying any further out of fear it would upset him, and I didn't want the girls to witness that. After breakfast, we spent the rest of our time driving down the old country roads of my past. When it was time to bring Daddy back, I debated with myself whether or not I would ever see him again. I didn't know if I wanted to have a relationship with him after that comment. I feared he didn't have remorse and that's not something I could deal with at the time.

I felt a sense of relief when it was time to bring Daddy back to the hospital. I realized I was not in the right state of mind to rekindle a relationship with him at that time. I was too fragile, too symptomatic, and just not in a good place.

CHAPTER SEVENTEEN:
SUICIDAL IDEATIONS

"Yvonne, are you okay? Can you hear me?" I heard an unfamiliar voice say.

Lying in the bed, I glanced over to see my husband standing beside a paramedic's crew surrounding me in our master bedroom. *Was I okay?* Of course, I was. I was finally sleeping after a daunting day of flashbacks. *Why in the hell did I have paramedics around me? Why did these jerks come along and wake me up?* I took a few pills that afternoon, but my intention wasn't to kill myself. It was to sleep. It was to numb the inundation of feelings that rushed back to me, like rainwater from a broken dam. I'd spent years keeping these feelings to myself, and now the atrocious memories resurfacing was too much for me to manage. I just wanted to go to sleep and wake up refreshed and feeling better. Instead, I awoke to paramedics poking and prodding me while loading me onto a stretcher.

"Why am I on a stretcher?" I asked.

"We need to get you checked out to make sure you're okay."

"But I feel fine. Is this necessary?"

"I'm sorry, but it is," Gavin interjected. "We have to be sure, baby, that's all."

"Okay, I'll go."

Gavin agreed to follow along behind.

The ambulance ride was quiet as I gazed out the window, wondering how long I'd have to be at the hospital. I didn't realize it would be a one-way trip that night. When paramedics rolled me in, I didn't go to an ordinary hospital room; they placed me in a room that looked more like a jail cell and locked me inside. The sound of the metal door slamming shut sent my anxiety through the roof, and I bawled.

"What is happening right now?" I asked through sobs.

"We need you to wait here until the psychiatrist can evaluate you," explained the nurse.

"Psychiatrist? I thought I was here to see a medical doctor."

"You will see both. The psychiatrist will decide how long you need to stay with us."

"What do you mean, how long? I want my husband right now. Where's my husband?" I screamed out in distress.

"He hasn't come in yet, but we'll bring him in as soon as he arrives. Right now, we need you to change into this hospital gown."

The room was stark and cold with a trace of antiseptics in the air. I wept uncontrollably, livid that everyone lied to me, and my anger monster returned. I screamed at everyone who came into my room, including Gavin.

"Gavin, how can you let them do this to me?" I asked through sobs.

Gavin was visually distressed. "This is out of my control, honey. My heart is breaking right now."

"I want to go home, baby. I just want to go home," I moaned.

"I know you do, baby. I want you to come home, but this is out of our control now."

I hugged him tightly, hoping that he would appeal to the doctors to release me into his custody. A few minutes later, an older, slender man with glasses entered the room and introduced himself as the psychiatrist on duty.

"What happened today?" he inquired.

"I accidentally took too many pills. I'm exhausted. I'm not sleeping at night and wanted to take a nap. I took the pills to help me fall asleep. That's it. I promise."

I was not too fond of the psychiatrist's bedside manner. He rudely responded that many people used the excuse of needing help sleeping when trying to take their own lives.

"I TOLD YOU I WASN'T TRYING TO KILL MYSELF!" I yelled at the top of my lungs.

"I don't appreciate you speaking to me in that manner," warned the psychiatrist.

"I don't appreciate you calling me a liar!" I yelled back. "Everyone keeps lying to me! The paramedics told me I was here to get a checkup and then go home."

"You're not going home tonight."

"What? Baby, please tell him it was an accident."

I begged Gavin to stand up for me, but the psychiatrist just wasn't having it.

"I've made my decision," the psychiatrist snapped as he walked out of the room, locking Gavin and me inside.

I felt helpless and betrayed by the authorities. How could they blatantly lie to me? The entire situation felt like the ultimate disregard for my feelings. How could they not see that their actions triggered me more?

I talked to anyone who would listen and told them this was all a mistake and not a suicide attempt. "This was all an accident, I promise," I pleaded, but the doctors didn't believe me and used the Baker Act to admit me. A Baker Act allows a facility to hold someone involuntarily out of fear they will harm themselves. Being in the ER after taking a handful of different pills didn't look right, so they kept me. The statute said they could hold me for up to seventy-two hours. First, I'd go to another facility, where I'd have a mental evaluation from their resident psychiatrist.

I got back into the ambulance and went to the facility, still hopeful that I'd be able to go home that night. I was sure I'd be able to talk to the psychiatrist right away and get everything straightened out. I was extremely apprehensive as I made my way from the facility triage to the communal area for patients. I didn't know how to act around the other patients. Should I speak to anyone? Keep my distance? Should I let my real pain be known, or pretend like everything was going to be okay? I did what I've always done. I convinced myself that everything was going to be okay and acted like nothing was wrong with me.

At the time, I convinced myself that I didn't know I swallowed a near-fatal number of pills. I told myself and anyone who would listen that I was just trying to fall asleep, but really, I wanted to numb all the emotional pain I was experiencing. Because of the depression, I felt like a worthless burden destroying Gavin and my girls' lives. I believed that the girls would be better off without their pathetic, depressed mom holed up in the bedroom in three-day-old clothes. I felt it would be healthier for me to be gone forever than have the girls deal with me in this mental state of depression. They deserved so much better than that.

The common room of the psychiatric ward was small and bland. There were two long tables pressed against the eggshell-white walls, a dozen wooden armchairs with orange pad cushions, and a 32-inch television mounted on the wall. I started by skimming the room for the "safe" people to befriend. If you asked me now, I couldn't tell you their names, but at the time, I wanted to know everything about them. I also knew that appearances were everything, so I was going to be the happiest "suicidal" person they'd ever seen. The psychiatrist on duty would discern I wasn't suicidal at all. They'd figure out I was okay and let me go home, but to my dismay, the psychiatrist had left for the day. I wouldn't be going back with my husband, but he promised to return the very next morning. I was terrified, held against my will, and there was nothing anyone could do about it.

The following morning, I waited impatiently for the psychiatrist to make his rounds. I needed to persuade him that I didn't belong there. I was happy and in a supportive relationship with a great husband and could care for my daughters who were twelve and fourteen at the time. As tricky as the flashbacks and nightmares were, I'd never try to take my life. It was all a misunderstanding and a waste of their time that I was even there. Besides, my husband was on his way, and together we'd talk him into releasing me.

I was so happy to see Gavin walk through the door. Finally, I wasn't alone. I ran to him and wrapped my arms around him. The safest place in the world was his arms. I knew it was all going to be okay because he was there. We were in the middle of an embrace when the psychiatrist walked into the room. We looked over at him nervously, like two teenagers caught making out.

"I see you two worked everything out," he said.

I looked at him perplexed, and then realized he assumed Gavin and I were at odds.

Gavin spoke up, "We're just ready for her to be home." I squeezed his hand in approval.

"Let's have a chat about that," the psychiatrist said as he led us to a table tucked away in the corner. "So, what happened last night?"

"I accidentally took too many pills."

"Did you try to kill yourself?"

"Absolutely not," I responded.

The doctor shifted his attention to Gavin. "What do you remember?"

"She wouldn't wake up, so I panicked and called 911."

Gavin stayed resolute and made it clear it was safe for me to return with him.

"I'm going to take her home and keep a close eye on her. I'll start monitoring all of her medication."

The doctor agreed to that course of action and made Gavin agree he would take responsibility for doling out my medication every day. Gavin agreed without hesitation, but it left me feeling more helpless. We reviewed my medication schedule and waited as the doctor jotted down a few notes. His face was expressionless, so I felt like I needed to make a final plea.

"I'm really okay, sir," I blurted out.

"That's good to hear," he responded.

Finally, after more than twenty-four hours, I left the hospital. As Gavin drove us home, we talked about my scary ordeal.

"Baby, I'm so glad you're coming home. I didn't sleep at all last night."

"You're telling me?" I responded sarcastically.

"I've been waiting here since six a.m. How was your night? Did you meet anyone?" Gavin asked.

"Eh, it was a typical night of nightmares. I woke up screaming several times. It was one of the worst nights of my life."

"I sat by the phone the whole time just in case you called," he said.

"I just can't wait to be home and hope I never have to go through that again."

By the time we made it to our house, Gavin believed the whole thing was an accident, and so did I. The truth is, it was a failed suicide attempt, and I'm thankful to be alive. It was the only way to express the anguish I felt deep inside from my past traumas that a month of therapy had swirling around in my soul. At that moment, I believed my family would be better off without me. I didn't want him to know the truth about how much I was hurting because I didn't think he'd understand. How could he?

After discussing it with Gavin and Laura, I decided to spend some time in an in-patient treatment facility in New Orleans. The insurance company would decide the length of my stay. I was grateful for the referral from Laura. It gave me a couple of weeks to focus on myself, and I came home with grounding tools to help me remain present in the here and now when I wanted to dissociate. Tools like naming five things I can see, four things I can smell, and three things I can touch. These tools still help me to this day to come to terms with the long road of therapy still ahead of me, but inpatient treatment taught me that I wasn't always aware of the dangers around me as a kid, and it wasn't up to me to protect myself.

It took a long time to understand that I jammed my pain down deep, thinking it would disappear, but it never went away. It just lodged itself so far in the back of my mind that it'd take over thirty years to feel it. That's the thing about emotional anguish. It lies dormant, waiting to rouse again when you least expect it.

I have good days, bad days, okay days, horrible days, and then there are overwhelmingly devastating days. Sometimes I'm wrecked by my lack of productivity around the house; my inability to contribute financially made me feel worthless and useless when others think they know what I should be doing with my time. On one of the worst days, it was more than just a crummy day. It seemed like my support system was crashing down. Family all around me implied my time to heal had expired, and I needed to get up, brush myself off, and get on with life already. What no one understood was that's how I lived my entire life. I spent more than thirty years suppressing terrible images, pushing the accompanying emotions deep down, and pretending everything was fine. I didn't suffer from mental pain alone. Physical pain started creeping up as well. I had severe stomach pain, tooth pain, and frequent dizziness. A review of my labs from my hospital stay showed quite a few abnormalities in some blood tests that needed specialist treatment. The compounding physical pain on top of the emotional torment made life exhausting for me.

Thankfully, the girls were with Brent, because it got worse when doctors admitted me back into the hospital for a week, for thrombocytopenia (low blood platelets) just a few weeks after my suicide attempt. They suspected a rare condition called porphyria (a group of liver disorders) and started me on excruciatingly painful treatments that involved the transfer of hemin (iron-holding porphyrin) into my bloodstream intravenously. After a few days of treatment, my platelet levels were still low, and my arm was quadruple the regular size. The results from a bone marrow biopsy came in the following day but offered no clues. My doctor released me the next day without a diagnosis. I felt drained and ornery from spending a week in the hospital and still not having answers for my symptoms.

When Gavin and I arrived home, the sun was shining, and the sky was blue, but by noon, the sky turned dark and stormy, and I was not ready for the cyclone of emotions that was coming straight for me. By nightfall, the clouds exploded into torrential downpours, etching the worst day of my life into the chapters of my history book forever. Gavin left home to grocery shop while I stayed behind to rest. I enjoy singing a great deal and use it to manage the turmoil of my emotions and pain. When Gavin left, the house fell quiet, and I started to sing. As the air in the room vibrated with the echoes of my painful past, tears slowly slid down my cheeks. I dug in deep and let the lyrics flow despite the vulnerability I felt inside. Amid my expression of deep pain, I heard a voice from the corner say, "Stop feeling sorry for yourself."

Chris is Gavin's brother and was our roommate at the time. I thought he was out for the day, so his voice jarred me, and I turned around to find him standing in his bedroom doorway.

"How can you be so insensitive?" I asked.

"You're not doing enough to get better. Stop crying and start doing something."

My face flushed blood red, and I exploded. "I'm not doing enough? I go to therapy twice a week, take my medications, and do my best to survive right now. What else do you expect me to do?"

Who does he think he is? Suddenly, I realized he was utterly unable to relate because he had no idea what I was going through. In the two years we'd been roommates, this was our first and only disagreement. I knew it was all a misunderstanding, but he didn't like that I raised my voice and abruptly left the house, which was fine with me because I just wanted to be alone. I knew we'd work it out when he got home, and we did.

I still felt dazed by the tiff with Chris but slowly started coming down. Less than twenty minutes after Chris stormed out, the front door burst open, and Gavin stomped through the house, visibly upset. So much already happened in such a brief period of time that I was physically and mentally exhausted. I took a deep breath before checking in with Gavin.

"Hey, baby, is everything okay?" I asked inquisitively.

"No, it's not okay. Why are you friends with your ex on social media?"

I knew exactly who he was talking about.

"He's not an ex. I thought we moved past this. I distinctly remember you telling me you were okay with our friendship."

"That's not what I said at all. I remember you agreed that it was inappropriate to be friends with our exes on social media."

Did he forget the hour-long therapy session we had with Laura discussing this very issue?

"Are you being serious right now? Is this really what you want to argue about?"

"I want to know why you added him."

"Baby, good God, I didn't realize it was so important. When are you going to learn to trust me?"

"It's not about trust; it's about keeping our word to each other."

Gavin's jealousy rarely got the best of him, but it did this night. We continued bickering in circles, until I eventually retreated to my corner of the bedroom. Today just wasn't a good day. After getting comfortable in my "spot" on the bed, I logged into my account to remove the offending online friendship. Within minutes of signing on, I received a direct message from a family member urging me to "Get off social media and get back to work!" *What is going on?* I thought. Have these people lost their minds? I'd just gotten home from the hospital that day and needed more time to recuperate. Why are they pushing me this way? Wasn't I doing enough? I felt guilty and ashamed that I didn't do more around the house, and feelings of inadequacy came roaring to the surface. The straw that broke the camel's back came later in the night when I received a second message from a different close family member, implying again that I was spending too much time on social media. They knew everything I was going through, so I didn't understand why they would pressure me so much.

After an emotional day of fighting with Gavin and Chris, I didn't have the stomach for one more criticism. That moment of emotional instability sent me over the edge, and I'd had enough.

"I can't take this anymore!" I screamed as I threw my purple plush blanket aside and stomped down the stairs to where Gavin was watching TV.

"What the fuck is wrong with everyone today?" I screamed.

"What? What's wrong?" Gavin asked with an attitude.

"Fucking family, that's what's wrong."

"What happened?"

"I've received two messages today commenting about my social media use, and I'm fucking sick of it! Everybody is on my back, and I just can't take it anymore. I need to get the fuck out of here for a while."

I slipped into my black flip-flops and stormed out the front door. I didn't know where I was going, but I needed to get away. I took off on foot, headed for our community gate exit. It was late, but I didn't care. I heard thunder in the distance, but not even that was going to turn me around. My phone rang.

"Where are you?" Gavin asked.

I answered him with the one thing that would make him feel the way I felt all day—hopeless, helpless, and out of control.

"I'm going to the bridge, and I'm going to jump," I said hastily.

"Baby come back. Let's talk about this."

"I'm done, Gavin. Please kiss the girls for me and tell them I love them. I can't take this anymore. I love you, but I'm going to jump off the bridge. I love you so much. Goodbye." And I hung up.

Gavin tried to call back, and I ignored his call. I knew I'd calm down by the time I got to the bridge, but it was the only way to express how much pain I was experiencing. Gavin called again, and I answered.

"What do you want, Gavin?"

"I want you to stop where you are. I'm coming after you."

"I can't take this, Gavin. I can't take your lack of trust, the family's harassment, and everyone being on me all in one day."

"I understand, baby, just calm down, and we can talk about this."

I refused and continued walking the few blocks to the I-75 bridge. I didn't know how to communicate that I was feeling rushed to "get better." I was just trying to communicate that I was in a lot of pain and felt pressured by those around me. Did everyone forget this journey is a marathon, not a sprint? I needed time to work through the remnants of my past. I felt worthless, helpless, and out of control of my life. I needed Gavin to understand that I was doing my best and defend me to anyone who said anything otherwise. I was so upset that the thought of calling Laura didn't even cross my mind.

I was sitting on the bridge railing, watching cars pass on the highway underneath, when it started to rain. My conniption was over, so I stood up and began walking back to the house. Suddenly, blue lights blinded me as they pulled over to the side of the road. I thought, *Shit, Gavin called the police.* I cooperated with the officer's commands and sat on the side of the road. This first police officer was compassionate and understanding.

"It's safe to tell me what's happening," the officer started.

"If I tell you what happened, will you just let me go home with my husband?" I asked.

"Just tell me why you walked out to the bridge tonight."

I looked around but I didn't see Gavin anywhere. I turned my attention back to the officer when a second squad car came onto the scene.

"I'll tell you if you assure me that I can go home with my husband after."

"Just be honest, and you can go home with your husband."

His reassurance relieved me because I didn't want to go back to that psychiatric hospital.

"I threatened to jump off the bridge because I was angry, but I'd never go through with it."

He seemed receptive to me, but when the second and third police officers showed up, the tone shifted dramatically. Police surrounded me, each of them asking questions, so I tried to explain.

"I'm just having a stressful day. Everyone is on my ass, and I had a moment, but I'm feeling better now," I explained. "I just got home from a weeklong hospital stay, so I'm sore from all the treatments. I'm also working on some deep issues in psychotherapy twice a week. I'm just exhausted and in constant pain."

The first officer empathized with me, but the second officer seemed to be having a difficult day himself, and I became the target of his frustration. The rain started falling a little harder, so the second officer led me to the back of his police car, where I'd be out of the storm.

"Can I talk to my husband, please?" I asked.

"Not right now."

"Sir, can you please explain to me what's going on?"

"My colleagues and I are trying to figure that out. Stay here for a minute. Please put your feet in the car so that I can close the door."

I pulled my feet inside, and he closed the door. I watched as the two officers talked briefly and then motioned for Gavin to come over. He'd been standing in the rain waiting for the officers to talk to him. When Gavin stepped into the light, he looked disheveled and anxious. After about 10 minutes, the second officer walked back to the cruiser, opened my door, and asked me to step out. I thought the whole thing was over, and I'd go home. Instead, as I stepped out of the vehicle, the third officer turned me around, slapped handcuffs on me, and escorted me to another car.

"What's happening?" I nodded at the first police officer. "He said I'd go home with my husband."

"Well, plans changed," the officer responded sarcastically.

"Gavin, please don't let them take me away. Please!" I begged.

Gavin stood helpless with tears in his eyes. He knew everything was out of his control.

"I'm going to find out what's happening, baby. Don't worry," Gavin yelled as I walked to the police car.

"Sir, please. I'm begging you, please just let me go home. These handcuffs are triggering me and making things so much worse." I just needed my arms in front of me. "Can I please put my arms in front of me?"

"No," the officer responded coldly, and my anger monster returned vigorously.

"You like handcuffing women, don't you? Does it make you feel like a real man?" I ranted.

The officer ignored me and guided me into the back of his vehicle. I made a last attempt. "Sir, PLEASE! I promise I just need to be with my husband. The handcuffs are triggering my anger. Please just cuff my hands in the front."

My pleas didn't move the officer, and he slammed the door. That's when panic washed over my body, and the anger monster took over.

"You're a fucking pussy! You don't have anything better to do?" I taunted. "How does it feel to trigger my C-PTSD and not give a shit about it? What a piece of shit you are."

The officer stayed silent as I criticized him and called him every name in the book the entire ride to the hospital. Looking back,

I'm lucky he didn't arrest me instead. He ushered me into the hospital, and again, placed me in a locked room.

"She's here for the night," I heard the officer tell a nurse before leaving.

"Fucking asshole!" I screamed out, hoping he heard before the door closed behind him.

No one cared about how I felt. This officer did the exact opposite of everything the others had promised me. Instead of confronting me with compassion and empathy, they treated me like a criminal. I was sick of people lying to me. The police officer said Gavin was on his way and would bring me home, but it was a lie.

I thought I could trust these people because of their profession, but I felt betrayed. It's difficult to characterize the anger I experienced. The frustration from the officer betrayal is indescribable. I thought he'd understand what I was going through, but he punished me for it instead.

My husband showed up at the hospital, but I wasn't going back home with him. Once again, the hospital used the Baker Act to keep me there, and I headed to the psychiatric unit for "observation." Each lie enraged me. How could the police lie to my face like that? The feeling of cold handcuffs made me shiver to my bones, and no one cared. The nurse assured me the doctor on staff would see me that day. He could rescind the Baker Act, suggesting that I may be able to go home that evening. Finally, I felt hopeful when Gavin arrived to speak to the doctor and sort this whole mess out.

After changing into a hospital gown, I sat at the end of the hospital bed swaying my legs back and forth, anxiously awaiting to speak with the doctor. After a few minutes there was a knock at the door and the physician on duty introduced himself as Dr. X and I immediately sensed he was cold and aloof. I twisted my long hair into a makeshift bun, like I was preparing for a fight. Within seconds of "evaluating" me, the doctor made up his mind.

"I'm not rescinding this Baker Act," he said as he put his pen back in the pocket of his white doctor's coat.

I was beside myself. "How can you come to that determination without even speaking to me first?" I asked. "This is incredibly insensitive of you!" I said with a dramatic kick to the bottom of the hospital bed.

He was as cold as his eyes and simply responded, "I've never rescinded a Baker Act and don't plan to start a new trend tonight."

And with that, he left the room, allowing the sturdy hospital door to slam shut behind him, and any glimmer of hope walked out the door with him. I was distraught and knew I wasn't going home that night. I understand caution, but this doctor was cold and mean. He didn't want to hear anything I said. It made me feel insane. I felt trapped. No one seemed to care that their actions made the situation worse. All I needed was to talk to someone and explain my side of the story. I called Laura, but sadly, there was nothing she could do.

Over the next few hours, my husband and I tried to get me released. I did my best to show I was in the wrong place. I became friendly with the staff, offered support to a couple of people I met, and laughed as much as possible, but to no avail. I stayed there until doctors released me the next afternoon. Although I felt extremely irked at the time, looking back, I understand the need to keep me for observation since, according to://www.webmd.com/mental-health /recognizing-suicidal-behavior, fifty to seventy-five percent of people who threaten suicide do try it. However, I still believe and stand by my opinion that there was no excuse for the police officer's lack of compassion or concern for my mental health in the process.

Weeks after returning home, people around me recommended that I "get up" and get "back to normal," while my therapist guided me to dig deeper into the vault of my hidden consciousness so I could release all the negative emotions attached to them. I'd been searching for a voice to express myself. Some days I erupted in joyful music; some days, I replaced music with silence. Sometimes I danced, sometimes I frantically paced the floor. Sometimes, I still have obsessive thoughts that trap me like a bad movie trailer on repeat. Other days, my brain won't let me in. It's as though a fog dominates my consciousness, and my mind goes into a deep void of dissociation to detach from the pain.

I didn't know how deep the pain went or if it would ever go away. I'd never delved so deep or allowed myself to feel so much discomfort, but for the first time, I felt optimistic that my childhood didn't permanently damage me. I remained hopeful that I was capable of exploring all my emotions in a healthy way while learning better ways to cope. From that day forward, my only ambition was to heal from my past.

CHAPTER EIGHTEEN:
REFLECTIONS

I realized that if I had any chance of being happy at all, I'd have to give in to the healing process. I knew unburdening my past through therapy was the only path to laughter, self-love, awareness, and happiness. Sometimes, we just need extra reassurance. We need to know everything is going to be okay. We need to feel safe enough to wax and wane with the flow of our emotions. That vulnerability is an inevitable part of healing that no one can ignore. I had that opportunity, thanks to Gavin and Laura's support. I had the time to discover who I am for the first time in my life and move forward from my past. I stepped out of a world that was once so clear into one that seemed unfamiliar. I'm learning new ways to live a life full of love, laughter, and family.

My fight-or-flight trigger switched to "high" during my very first trauma at four years old, and it would come back to haunt me later in the form of repetition compulsions. The urge is strongest when things are going really well in life because living comfortably felt unfamiliar to me as a child. I realize now that I wasn't putting myself in potentially harmful situations because I wanted it; I was merely acting out from all my childhood traumas because of repetition compulsion. Due to years of abuse and neglect, I believed in a distorted version of what a healthy life looked like before starting therapy. From birth to the age of ten, my parents exposed me to daily raging violence. I experienced the worst type of betrayal repeatedly, the betrayal of neglect from my parents for their lack of protection. My war began at the age of four, and I continued to struggle more than thirty years later.

I've carried a lot of guilt, blame, and shame over the years when most of it didn't belong to me. I've beat myself up for putting myself in dangerous situations, but the reality is, I can't control another person's actions. I'm not responsible for what a person does to me. I can only control myself. I've learned that motive is everything. It's how I've learned to distinguish the good from the bad and the evil from the ignorant and to make sense of the immense guilt I harbor for my poor judgment.

I spent years acting out because of my abuse. I sought love and attention from men in positions of power and abusive relationships. I allowed men to use me, make me their sexual object, and force me to do things I never thought I'd do. From the sadistic to the disgusting, I've seen it all (thankfully, I haven't done it all). I never learned from the women in my orbit that I deserved respect, so I had to learn how to become the strong woman I desperately needed as a child. I now know that self-value comes from within, and I've fought hard to build it up.

Because of my dysfunctional upbringing, I didn't know a friend from a foe, but I grew to believe that anyone in a powerful position cared about me. Later in life, I found myself blindly trusting people due to my misguided belief that they cared about me, and I could trust them with my psychological well-being. My perspective about that has completely changed. The truth is, more than one person in a position of power has shattered my boundaries, proving they don't care about me at all. You can't trust anyone who doesn't set firm boundaries. If someone tells you your trust is in the right place, then chances are, it isn't. I learned I can't control how people treat me. This mistake set off a repetition compulsion cycle that lasted for years. All because I thought I could stop the compulsive thoughts meandering in my head by sharing them with a person in power. It was an emotionally and psychologically harmful blunder.

Some people played a dangerous game with my psychological well-being for their cheap thrill. The lack of boundary-setting made messages ambiguous and triggered the deep confusion I felt when I was with Craig. I didn't know if he was playing a game with me. Was he playing hard to get or keeping his distance? It's hard to distinguish during repetition cycle, especially when boundaries aren't set. I continued pursuing friendships because my behavior was rewarding my negative self-belief. This cycle perpetuated the belief that I'm only interesting if I'm sexual or I'm worthless and nobody cares about me. It's a vicious, vicious cycle that hopefully, awareness can help me avoid in the future.

The most important lesson I learned from the people around me was that I didn't want my life to be anything like theirs. Therapy was giving me a renewed sense of self. I could feel myself growing. I was even starting to bloom, but my memories were weeds in my beautiful garden, and I wanted them out. I often asked myself, how in the hell did I survive my childhood? I have such a beautiful life now considering my upbringing, but how did that happen? How did I escape being just another statistic of drug addiction? Prostitution? These thoughts were as random as the wind, and the answer felt meaningless. As a child, I thought the answer was forgiveness.

Mama raised me to believe that everyone is a sinner, and all sinners deserve forgiveness no matter what. My family believes that forgiveness is necessary in the eyes of God, and only he can judge others for their actions. Imagine how confusing those contradictory beliefs are for a child. My family couldn't judge pedophiles but would quickly label a stranger a "whore" if they didn't approve of their clothing choice. Mama taught me that forgiving others was best for me, and if I forgave all the perpetrators who tortured me, I'd find peace.

Therapy has taught me that Mama's beliefs on forgiveness couldn't be more deluded. I realize people must earn my forgiveness, much like respect and trust. Forgiveness is for the survivor and is a process of working through the feelings and aftereffects of their trauma. Only then can the survivor truly decide to forgive or not; either way, it's their choice. A person deserves forgiveness when they can take responsibility for their actions and change their future behaviors. I've learned that incest and mental illness run deep on both sides of my genealogy, but more so on Mama's side. I don't know how far back this generational curse goes on, but I yearned to bring the vicious cycle to a screeching halt for my own family. I'm launching my effort through bringing awareness to a problem that generations of families have minimized and swept under the rug.

I'm suffering deeply now because I never had the opportunity to process years of righteous anger and emotional pain from my traumas. I used forgiveness to stay in denial about the chaos around me. This illusion of forgiveness only caused me to suppress unhealthy feelings that I should've been able to express as a child. I never let anyone know I was in pain. Anytime anyone saw me, I'd have a big smile on my face. I wanted to make people feel good and became a people pleaser.

In therapy, I learned my childhood experiences distorted my idea of "love," which made me vulnerable to predators like Justin and Craig. I was a habitual girlfriend. I jumped from relationship to relationship, searching for something different. I was searching for happiness from others when happiness can only come from within myself. I've been longing for stability since I was a little girl and latched on to any person who I thought could provide that.

Codependency was one of my responses to my multiple traumas. Justin and Craig physically, sexually, verbally, and mentally abused me, yet I didn't want to leave their sides. I lost sight of my happiness by focusing all my attention on making them happy somehow. I willingly sacrificed the treatment I knew I deserved for the off-chance possibility that they would change. I believed so deeply that if I loved them enough, they'd want to be a better man to me, and be mine forever.

I'm learning that words are meaningless. Just because someone says "I love you" doesn't mean they do. Craig had a way of painting the most beautiful picture with his words, but his actions spoke of darkness, pain, and humiliation. He would tell me how much he respected me but then be incredibly disrespectful toward me. Craig said he needed me yet would refuse to speak to me until I agreed to his request. He'd say he hated the idea of being with others, then call me weak and incapable of being who he wanted me to be when I'd balk. His actions didn't match the words.

Being in a long-term abusive relationship can affect people in unusual ways. For me, it was difficult for me to leave because I felt unlovable. The abuse stripped away my confidence in myself and sometimes made me feel helpless. Others have difficulty leaving an abusive relationship because their abuser controls the finances, and they simply don't have the resources. I've learned that there are many resources available to help victims get out of their dangerous situations.

Looking back, I now realize the affair with Craig didn't bloom out of physical attraction. It blossomed out of calculated lies, compliments, emotional manipulation, mind control, and my sincere desire for someone to love me. He won me over with flattery, plain and simple. His words, in the beginning, made me feel things I'd never felt before. I felt beautiful, intelligent, and most of all, special. He was the first ever to express his undying love for me, and I soaked it all in, not knowing it would turn out to be toxic lies. I once considered this relationship to be just another mistake in my book, but at the time, my need for love stemmed from the deep psychological trauma from my childhood.

One of the most confusing things for me to grapple with is the idea that things aren't always as they seem. It feels like the trigger of my repetition compulsion is about the person who triggered it. Past trauma drives every trigger or anxiety inducer or repetition compulsion and is extremely difficult to experience. It's a serious unconscious aftereffect that can plague someone for years. We are all human and just want to feel camaraderie with other humans like everyone else. My abandonment caused me to seek out camaraderie from others to fill the void from familial connections I lacked as a child.

I still look for the best in people, but I try to remember all the wolves in sheep's clothing I've met and then recognize that things aren't always as they appear. People can be cruel, thoughtless, and devoid of empathy. They can smile in your face and tell you they are your friend, and then turn on you on a dime when you no longer serve their purpose. I'm better prepared for it now. I'm more aware. People who seem "normal" sometimes pose the most significant threat.

The only person I have the power to control is myself. If someone isn't being clear with me about their boundaries, I ask for clarification, especially with people in a position of power. I learned I have the right to know where I stand with others, and they have the right (and duty) to set and keep strict boundaries. I blamed myself for what happened with Craig, but I now know I had no control over his behavior, even though at the time, I felt like a complete failure. The only thing I'm to blame for is blindly trusting that man.

As a caretaker, I naturally put my boundaries aside for others, hoping for reciprocation. I still struggle with this from time to time and continue to learn how to honor the boundaries I deserve, including a healthy amount of self-care. I've cultivated "me" time that I cherish. I started with exercise, and now I've added bubble baths and a skincare regime to my weekly routine. Some days are still better than others, and I turn to my husband or therapist for the extra support I need.

I somehow became both affectively and cognitively empathetic without anyone being understanding of my needs. I believe it could be a skill my psyche needed to develop to make sense of the nonsense I endured for so many years. I've learned not to jump to conclusions about anyone, good or bad. I've learned to put myself in others' shoes to see things from their perspective, which taught me how to be a reflective person myself.

Therapy is helping me understand my compulsion to repeatedly put myself in similar situations with people in positions of power. These past six years in treatment have been earth-shattering in the best ways. I've learned that due to the absence of my father in my life, I was more vulnerable to find myself in inappropriate situations where I could repeat a past trauma. Although this is a normal, predictable aftereffect of trauma, neglect, and abuse, it's exceedingly difficult to control without psychotherapy. I didn't realize this during my marriage to Brent. Looking back, I knew we had a loveless marriage, and I subconsciously wanted it to end.

I'm learning how to identify my feelings and communicate my needs effectively. It's because of these brand-new communication skills that I have such a solid foundation with Gavin and my daughters. I've learned new ways to cope with painful memories or feelings that come up. Communication is the key to healing. I'm learning it's okay to feel bad from a sad moment or memory. We need to talk about our feelings and have open communication.

Healing has helped me realize it's okay for my daughters to know about my depression because I'm modeling good self-care and attend therapy regularly. I know I'm doing my absolute best to get better, and so do my children. Communication about these things is so important. Breaking the stigma related to depression teaches our younger generation a healthier way to manage their sad feelings.

Nowadays, I'm better aware of what triggers my repetition compulsions and can discuss it openly with Gavin and Laura. We talk about whatever the obsessive thoughts and negative aftereffects are that have controlled my decision-making process for many years. Before therapy, I rarely felt "normal" in most social interactions. I stayed inside my shell fearing I had a mental defect everyone would find out about. Thanks to my work with Laura, I understand my trauma dumped C-PTSD onto an otherwise normal person. It's not something I was born with or a mental shortcoming.

Starting the therapeutic process isn't easy, but I now know it's okay to allow myself to go into that difficult space. That's where the healing begins. There's no shame in asking for professional help. I think everyone who's experienced trauma should have a therapist. But merely "going" to therapy is useless unless you are willing to put in the work it takes to truly heal and grow from all the traumatic events in your life.

Each place holds a secret; each location has a memory; each site has played a role in molding me into the woman I am today. I used to feel grateful for challenging times. I once felt blessed to have had the life experiences I've had, because I thought it made me stronger. I'd ask myself, "Who knows where I'd be if I didn't have the freedom to move to New Hampshire? Or to Florida? How could my life have turned out?" The truth is, I wouldn't have endured four years of torment by a drug-addicted sex offender if Mama didn't allow me to leave home at fifteen. New Hampshire was my escape plan, but I didn't speak to anyone in my family for years after moving. I was eighteen and entirely on my own. Out of sight, out of mind, as they say. I focused my energy on creating my own ways, my own path to success, learning from my mistakes, and celebrating my victories along the way. In the end, I'm the only person responsible for my inner happiness.

The most beautiful part about life is that we get to start over repeatedly. Each morning is a new gift. A unique opportunity to make the change we want to see in your lives. What happened yesterday doesn't matter. The only thing that matters is to be in the present. Appreciate the things you have and love the people in your life. Never stop giving up on your dreams and never be afraid to ask for what you want; the answer will always be "no" if you never ask. We all have the power to be anything we want to be. Our past doesn't define who we are. Your history doesn't make you who you are today; your strength does. Your past is nothing but a steppingstone to help guide you closer to your dream.

I've learned it's okay to put myself first. No matter how resilient I thought I was, I wouldn't have survived if I didn't deal with my past trauma and abuse. I had to accept that not even God can stop the aftereffects of childhood trauma. Prayer and faith can bring great peace and comfort, but not healing. The only way to heal is to confront your trauma and forgive yourself for your part in it. Forgiving yourself will create the space you need in your mind and soul to discover the magic in your life. We all have greatness inside. We just need to find it so that we can accept it. That's when you'll liberate yourself from your past. I'm taking one day at a time. No one can merely overcome their traumatic past; they must go through the healing process.

My mind is a powerful survival tool that helped me as a child and an adult. After starting treatment, lost memories rushed to the forefront of my mind, and the anguish of injustice surged through my body. No one ever faced prosecution for more than a dozen despicable crimes committed against me. Sometimes that fact is just too much to take. Therapy is helping me realize that healing is within reach. I just needed to gain the psychological tools to help me keep the trajectory going.

My journey is far from over after six years into therapy. Still, I vividly remember how difficult it was for me to step foot inside Laura's office. Now, well into my journey, I can't imagine my life without her. Therapy continues to have such a positive impact on my overall wellbeing. I was afraid to confront the overwhelming anguish from my childhood, but the gift of liberation I've received in return has been worth every second.

I learned the hard way that merely stepping into a therapist's office wouldn't solve my problems. It required an intense commitment and willingness to explore the deepest depths of my soul to reach the well of anguish I continue to drain week after week. Depression can hit you when you least expect it and often can happen when life is going great. That's what happened to me. Gavin made me feel so safe that the barrier I'd built up between me and my emotions came crashing down and the exploration of my feelings could begin.

Despite having an incredible husband, two amazing daughters, and a family that will do anything for me, sometimes, the righteous anger I have for others turns inward, and depression takes over. Still, it took immense strength to get to where I am today. Without therapy, I may have never discovered who I am, tamed irrational thoughts of worthlessness and blame, or morphed into the person I've always been meant to be. For that, I'm incredibly proud.

Over the years, Mama, my grandparents, and aunts and uncles all have said Mark is the "only father we've ever had," but not in any way that it counts. He put himself before his wife and stepchildren. Mark didn't show me the treatment women deserve. He showed me how some men like to disrespect and demean women. He taught me that when times get tough, you run. You replace your life and the people in it with what you think will be better. He taught me that some men are okay with not taking care of their families. Now two fathers had abandoned me. The only lesson I learned from Mark was the type of husband I didn't want. Both of my "fathers" showed characteristics that I never wanted my children to be around.

It took me a long time to accept my righteous anger at Mark. Mama always said he was the best dad I ever had, which I used to believe, but Mark didn't protect me as a father. He later admitted that he "heard something about" what Frank did to me and, once again, confirmed they were still friends. They are friends to this day. Mark didn't support our family and didn't take care of our basic needs. He brought heartbreak to our family. He cheated on Mama, abandoned us all, and broke our hearts. Mark isn't my stepdad anymore. They say you can't choose family but thank God we can get rid of the loose ends that only remind us of pain and resentment. Stepparents can be temporary. Thankfully for me, that's all he will ever be. Mama deserved much more than he gave. We all did.

I always missed my brothers and hoped they were okay. Some still harbor unresolved anger and have trouble controlling it. Mama would tell me about the holes they'd punch in walls and all the fights she had to break up when they were growing up. They're all grown now, but not much has changed for some, while everything has changed for others. Michael has completely turned his life around, but sadly, Christian still struggles with his rage. I recently asked Christian, now thirty-four, what he remembered about our childhood, and his answer broke my heart.

"I just remember roaming the streets," he said, in a very matter-of-fact way.

His answer almost brought me to tears because I know he meant it quite literally. He never had a father figure in his life, no one to guide him in the dark times, and Mama didn't shine a beacon of light for him to follow. I've come to accept that I can't change anyone, no matter how much I love them. Change comes from the individual and nowhere else. I wasted years trying to convince my immediate family that life doesn't have to be so complicated, but it's up to them to make it happen. My brothers are all in their thirties and forties and struggle with their own inner demons from our childhood. They all have children of their own that they've raised the best they can. I'm much closer with my brothers now, and I look forward to spending more time getting to know them as adults and can only hope they'll seek out the professional help they need when the time is right.

My dad is now in his own apartment and I'm proud to say that he's been sober since his stroke in 2014. In February 2020, I found the courage to confront him again about what he knew about my childhood, and he conceded to knowing about a molestation that occurred to me at five or six, but I don't recall the incident. I wonder if he was thinking about the incident with Trevor. It bothered me for a while, thinking there was a molestation that occurred that not even I can remember.

I learned I don't need my dad's validation to accept the traumas I experienced. It happened to me whether he remembers or not. And it happened because my parents abandoned me, including my father. I asked him why he didn't try to find us when we were younger, and he said he did. He told me Mama wouldn't let him see me. Was that her way of trying to protect us? If so, it made no sense. Why would she hide us, but not hesitate to send us to live with him when it was convenient for her? It's difficult for me to blame my dad when most of the sexual abuses and physical traumas I survived happened on Mama and Mark's watch. At the time, it felt overwhelming to think that this abusive, alcoholic man that brutally beat my mom regularly could protect me and support my needs better than Mama.

That one year my brothers and I lived with Dad, we had food, clothing, and shelter. We were in school full time and had the opportunity just to be kids, something none of us had before. Still, it's not "normal" for a parent to leave their thirteen-year-old and eleven-year-old home alone all night to care for a two- and four-year-old. Even though he wasn't perfect, it was better than any home I lived in with my mom and Mark, and that's painful to admit and greatly confusing.

I miss my dad. I need my dad as much as any other girl needs her father. The difference is, I've accepted that he'll never be the father I needed as a child, but we can create a new bond as adults. I'm unsure what the future holds for us, but our recent phone calls are a great start. We now talk a couple of times a month. He's asked for my forgiveness, but I'm not sure he knows all the things that require my absolution. He may be incapable of unpacking the many ways he failed as a father, but I appreciate that he is trying. We're slowly getting to know each other again.

I didn't have a relationship with my dad's parents at all until 1998, when Grandma reached out to me before she died of pancreatic cancer. I was eighteen and living in New Hampshire. I flew to Alabama to spend time with her two weeks before she passed. I rode along to help her, and Grandpa pick out linoleum for the kitchen. We spent the rest of the trip together at their house, chatting and catching up. She seemed kinder and gentler than I remembered, affectionate, and interested in my life. I regretted not connecting with her more, but therapy taught me that, as the adult, it was Grandma's job to keep up the relationship with me. It wasn't my failure; it was hers. She wasted precious time we could've spent together, questioning my paternity.

Still, if there's one relationship I could do over, it would be my relationship with my grandma. I learned that we both loved to sing, and our favorite flower was the rose. I can't help but wonder what a great childhood I may have had if that relationship had been different. I have four cousins on Dad's side who were extremely close with my grandparents because they grew up around them. I longed for that in my own life. The last photo Grandma and I took together is the only reminder I have of how much I look like her. That's the day she finally told me that she knew I was her granddaughter. After years of questioning my paternity, she couldn't deny it any longer because I looked just like her.

Mama has survived on disability since 2010 from an injury in a car accident. She's in her own home and recently bought Granny and Pawpaw's house. I've seen Mama multiple times, but she still struggles with distorted thinking and claims to be "over" her past, but I know that can't be true. She can't heal from a past she's not willing to confront. She still has a heart of gold and would give anyone the shirt off her back. Right now, I can't support a regular relationship with her because we're in various stages of healing. It will take a huge step of courage on her behalf for our healing as mother/daughter to begin. Until she chooses to get professional help through treatment, sadly, she'll never heal from her traumas.

I defended her for years because of the abuse she suffered. Now, I know that the abuse she sustained had nothing to do with her duty as a mother to protect me, and she let me down. I've only recently tapped into the righteous anger I have toward her, and as a mom myself, I can't fathom neglecting my children the way she grossly neglected me. I thought I'd forgiven her years ago, but time has shown that isn't true.

I recently asked Mama what she remembered about the day the men sliced themselves open, and she remembered things differently. She thought the owner put a gun to the dog's head and then said my brother and I weren't at the fire at all. It's incredible how two people have such different recollections of the same events. The healing process reminds me that sometimes people only remember what they want to remember because the truth is too painful to face. I did that for a long time. Now, I accept that their recollection doesn't change my reality.

I now realize that whatever happened to me in Trevor's trailer was a memory I safeguarded with years of repression. In a way, I protected my mother because, when brought to light, that memory would become blood on my Mama's hands, and they might never come clean. It devastated me that Mama didn't save me. I have no recollection of going home that day or where my brother was when it happened. Still, it doesn't matter because the event already caused damage to my psyche. Sexual trauma forever stained my four-year-old mind. I lost trust in the person who was supposed to protect me the most, my mother. My parents crossed my sexual boundary when they didn't protect me. It took me a long time to understand that mistake is an extension of the abuse. Not only was I abused by Trevor, Lou, Larry, Clarke, and others, but my parents compounded the trauma with their lack of allegiance to me.

Years later, I confronted my mom about how she remembered the day I tried to escape Trevor. And again, she remembers the morning quite differently. Mama said she heard me knocking, but her hands were wet from washing dishes. She looked out the window to see who was at the door. Mama saw Trevor holding me over his shoulder but denied knowing I was in danger. She thought we were just horsing around. How could she not know I needed help? I kicked, screamed, and cried out. What else could I have done to get through to her? I crammed anger down toward Mama for years. I directed it at myself and the monster who violated my body instead of letting her feel the wrath of my righteous anger for not coming to my aid.

Mama said I didn't tell her what happened to me until I was seven years old. She told me she took matters into her own hands when she enlisted a biker friend to "teach Trevor a lesson." She attests that several men tied him to a tree, beat him, and dropped him at the bus station with a warning: "Don't come back or you will die." According to Mama, he got on that bus, and she hasn't seen him since. I don't know the whole story, but her actions repeatedly showed me that she didn't react with the same ferocity when she came face to face with men that did much worse to me.

I love my mom and need her as much as I need my dad. Like my dad, I don't think I'll be able to fully forgive her until she takes accountability and seeks professional help for herself. It's the immense love that I have for my mom that is also the source of my deepest pain. Mama tells me she's proud of me all the time, but to me, those are empty words. She won't learn about all the traumas I've endured and the amount of burdensome work I've put in to get to where I am today. She can't begin to understand until she acknowledges all my traumas and takes accountability for her negligence over the years. Our recent conversations confirmed she has more work to do. They all go the same way.

"How are you doing?" Mama asks.

"I'm hanging in there. I've had a few tough therapy sessions lately, but I'm getting better every day."

"I'm happy to hear that. I can't begin to tell you how sorry I am for being a bad mother. I wish there were something I could do to fix it."

"Well, we can't change the past, but we can focus on our future. The best thing you can do to help me is get therapy for yourself to process all the traumas you've been through."

"I'm not worried about me, Eve. I'm worried about you. I'm over everything in my past."

"Oh, Mama, I wish that were true. You can't begin to help me until you heal yourself from all the guilt and shame you feel about it first. Therapy will help you process those feelings and come to terms with what transpired over the years."

"Therapy just isn't for me. I don't want to talk about the past. I'm over it."

This topic is always a point of frustration for me during our calls. I'm telling Mama precisely what I need when she asks, and she ignores it. The call always ends the same way it started.

"I'm glad we got to talk. I'm so proud of you, Eve. I'll do anything to make things right with you. I love you so much."

"The best way to help me is to start going to therapy. That's what I need from you. I love you, too."

And then nothing happens. Just more empty words.

Larry's ex-wife, Diane, admitted to me in 2016 that her son, RJ, demonstrated to her what "Daddy did to Eve" with two dolls, but she did nothing about it. I'll never understand how any adult could allow such travesties to continue. Why didn't anyone investigate or try to stop it? These questions hold answers I'll never know, but it doesn't erase the curiosity from my mind. The closest I got to an answer was when a fiery conversation about domestic violence in January 2021 opened the door for me to ask.

"There's always two sides to every story," Mama declared.

"That's not always true, Mama. A man never has the right to hit a woman, ever."

"You're always on the side of the victim, Eve."

I never imagined having the courage to directly confront my mom, but suddenly, I was saying things I needed to express to her since I was a child.

"How DARE you say that to me!" It was like a gut punch to the stomach. "You're always on the side of the perpetrator, Mama!"

I thought that would be enough, but I couldn't stop myself from continuing. "You never protected me, Mama! How could you remain friends with people that hurt me?" Before she had a chance to respond, I added, "Why haven't you confronted Diane about what she knew about my abuse as a kid?"

I paused long enough for Mama to cut in. I needed her to answer that question.

"Diane's been my best friend for thirty years, Eve."

"I've been your daughter for forty-one, Mama!" I screamed back. I repeated it to make sure she heard me. "I've been your daughter for forty-one years. How can you not be angry that she knew Larry abused me and did nothing about it?"

Now, Mama was on the defense. "I didn't know about it at the time, Eve."

Her response infuriated me more. I wanted to know about now, not then. "But you know about it now, Mama; why don't you call Diane to ask her about it now?"

"Because I don't like confrontation," she muttered.

"That's what I mean, Mama. How can you not be seething? How can you not be boiling over with so much anger that you can't stop yourself from confronting her?"

My rapid-fire questioning left her speechless for a moment.

"I just don't know where I was or how this happened, Eve. I don't understand why I stayed friends with Larry or allowed you to be around strangers. I can't handle all the grief from what happened to you," she confessed.

"Mama, if I can handle healing from what happened to me, you can handle knowing about it. Therapy can help you with that. That's why I've been begging you to go. Therapy will help you find the answers to all those questions and help you grieve and heal from those mistakes."

"I don't deserve to get better," Mama remarked.

"Mama, that's just the thing, you don't deserve to suffer. You deserve to heal from your pain."

Mama believed she was better serving me by suffering from her mistakes, rather than grieving and learning from them. It's hard for Mama to understand that I don't hate her. When I tell her I love her, she sometimes responds with, "I don't know why." She can't grapple with the fact that I can love her, because I'm healing from the pain she and others have caused me. The insights I've gotten in therapy have really opened my heart to forgiveness for her, but she must follow through with actional behavior to earn it back.

By the end of the call, Mama sorrowfully apologized multiple times, and I accepted. I hope she follows through with her promise to finally get the help she desperately needs. Time will tell, but I'm optimistic. That phone call was a great catalyst to getting us where we need to be. It was the first time Mama had expressed a genuine desire to heal. Our relationship is a work in progress. I realize from my own experience that forgiveness is part of the pathway to my healing. Knowing this, and not being there yet, tells me I have more healing to do. And I'll do what it takes because I want nothing more than to have that special bond a daughter has with her mom. It's been six long years of therapy, and I still have new insights into my healing every appointment and am confident that my bond with my mom will continue to strengthen.

Therapy has opened my eyes to a new way of life. I've become aware of my triggers, such as our current political environment, men in positions of power who don't set boundaries, visits with my family, news reports of molestation and abuse of children, to name a few, and the relentless aftereffects that haunt me from my past. As a child, I needed the coping mechanisms and distorted thinking to survive. My younger self couldn't make sense of the nonsense and used these coping skills and distorted thoughts to get through. Laura and all the other therapists I worked with during my in-patient treatment were kind and caring and knew how to guide me through my pain.

I'm working toward the healthiest defense mechanism of all—setting and keeping boundaries with those around me. I had to learn what my limits are by tuning in to my feelings. If I feel uncomfortable or resentful, I know I need to set better boundaries in a relationship. The empowerment to speak my voice is where the magic is starting to happen for me. Until now, I was passive. I'd take anything a person threw at me without expressing my feelings in return. It's not enough to just set boundaries—we must be assertive and follow through with them. Now, I'm direct about my needs and allow myself to set those boundaries. It all begins with being self-aware and accepting what I can and cannot control.

I now know that I was suffering from severe social anxiety, which stood in the way of new friendships. Because of my childhood trauma, I grew into an adult who trusted too easily, loved too freely, and allowed others to hurt me too often, but now I understand why. I trusted quickly because of my distorted belief that people deserve my trust until they break it. The truth is, someone has to earn my trust before I give it. I loved people too quickly because I wanted someone to love me. I believed if I felt it, the object of my affection must be feeling the same way. I laid my heart out in the open, then cried as people stepped on it. I allowed myself to hurt too often by caring about people who didn't care about me.

I'm acclimating to being selfish with my kindness unless someone has proven themselves worthy otherwise. The old me put up with anything in the name of trying to find something good in all people, despite so many proving there wasn't much "good" in my world. Still, the "old" me believed everything happened for a reason, but not because of a belief in God. The universe thrust upon me a more meaningful life lesson, which was to understand that sometimes things happen for no reason at all. The former me believed there's some lesson to gain from every trauma I endured, but sometimes there's no good reason for anything to happen, including the travesties I'd endured earlier in life. I tolerated the pain, thinking the cause was a lesson to learn. I concluded I needed to be kinder, more understanding, and patient with others' shortcomings in the hope they'd reciprocate.

I'm grateful to have an incredibly supportive husband, a loving, inclusive family, and two terrific daughters that make me so proud it brings tears to my eyes. After everything I've been through, I—and the two amazing men who help—have done a phenomenal job raising our girls. They're both so sweet, loving, intelligent, and talented. They're incredibly affectionate and bring joy to my life every day. We don't end a phone call without saying I love you or leave the house without a goodbye hug. These are all the things I longed for as a child. I'm so blessed to share this with my girls. They know I love them and will always fiercely defend and protect them from anything. As the years go by, I see them growing into their personalities and they make me laugh every day. I love our impromptu dance and karaoke nights. I love watching the joy on their faces when we celebrate their birthdays and spend holidays together. They're so free, so self-expressive, so special to me. They are living proof that survivors can raise smart, intelligent, and healthy children. Ashley is now nineteen and graduates from high school in May 2021. Claire is sixteen and learning how to drive. They both have therapists of their own. I didn't pass my psychological issues down to them. I compartmentalized my emotions to protect them at all costs. As the years in therapy go by, I don't have to do that as often. I can face my feelings as they come and know the moment is only temporary, and it too shall pass.

Gavin and I have been married six years, and I've never been happier. He's all-in on this journey with me and needed someone to help him understand this process and work on his own issues. He now sees a therapist of his own and says it's a "game-changer." He has been there for me during my darkest moments and never left my side. He goes out of his way to show me that he loves me and supports me every step of the way. He continually shows me the meaning of true love, and I absolutely love my life. I've come so far in my journey, and it's all because Gavin loved me enough to convince me to go to therapy. Our relationship gets stronger all the time, and we continue to help each other grow. I spent years fighting my way through the gloom for this. And it has been all worth it.

When I'm gone, I hope those who know me will reminisce over my love for hugs, karaoke, and dance parties. Commemorate how intensely I love my girls and how well I've raised them. Remember me as a kind, loving, enthusiastic, creative, and genuine person with art and a legacy to reflect on—someone who loves to laugh and make others laugh. Do not remember me as the invisible girl; remember me for the invincible woman I've become. I am a warrior, and that's something no one can ever take away from me.

RESOURCES

Lauren's Kids
Preventing Child Abuse – Healing Survivors
www.laurenskids.org

ChildHelp National Child Abuse Hotline
1-800-422-4453
https://www.childhelp.org/

The National Domestic Violence Hotline
1-800-799-7233
www.thehotline.org

The National Teen Dating Abuse Hotline – Love is Respect
1-866-331-9474
Text: 22522
https://www.loveisrespect.org/

Sexual Abuse Crisis Text Line
Text HOME to 741741 (US & Canada)

Text HOME to 85258 (UK)
Text HOME to 50808 (Ireland)
https://www.crisistextline.org/

Rape, Abuse, and Incest National Network (RAINN) –
National Sexual assault hotline
1-800-656-HOPE (4673)
www.rainn.org

National Human Trafficking Hotline
1-888-373-7888
Text: 233733
https://humantraffickinghotline.org/

StrongHearts Native Helpline
1-844-762-8483
www.strongheartshelpline.org

Pathways to Safety International
1-833-723-3833
E-mail: crisis@pathwaystosafety.org
https://pathwaystosafety.org/

The National Suicide Prevention Lifeline
1-800-273-8255
www.suicidepreventionlifeline.org

Gay, Lesbian, Bisexual and Transgender National Hotline
1-888-843-4564
Youth Talk line: 1-800-246-7743
Senior Helpline: 1 (888) 234 – 7243
Email: help@LGBThotline.org
http://www.glbtnationalhelpcenter.org/

Substance Abuse and Mental Health Services
Administration (SAMHSA)
1-800-622-HELP (4357)
www.samhsa.gov/find-help/national-helpline

Alcoholic Anonymous (AA)
1-800-839-1686
https://alcoholicsanonymous.com/

Narcotics Anonymous – Find a meeting (NA)
1-818-773.9999
https://www.na.org/meetingsearch/

ABOUT THE AUTHOR

 Yvonne Sandomir is a Cognitive Behavioral Life Coach. She has been a lifelong poet and became an author to elucidate the rampant epidemic of child sexual abuse in the United States. When Yvonne's not writing or in sessions with clients, you can find her singing karaoke, dancing around the house, painting, or spending lots of time with her husband and two daughters.